GW00645294

LETTINGS LAW

FOR PROPERTY PROFESSIONALS

Your Legal Questions Answered

Gina Peters

R^ethink

First published in Great Britain in 2022
by Rethink Press (www.rethinkpress.com)

© Copyright Gina Peters

All rights reserved. No part of this publication may be reproduced, stored in or introduced into a retrieval system, or transmitted, in any form, or by any means (electronic, mechanical, photocopying, recording or otherwise) without the prior written permission of the publisher.

The right of Gina Peters to be identified as the author of this work has been asserted by her in accordance with the Copyright, Designs and Patents Act 1988.

This book is sold subject to the condition that it shall not, by way of trade or otherwise, be lent, resold, hired out, or otherwise circulated without the publisher's prior consent in any form of binding or cover other than that in which it is published and without a similar condition including this condition being imposed on the subsequent purchaser.

Cover image © Shutterstock | Nizwa Design

Disclaimer

All thoughts and opinions are my own, unless attributed to alternative sources.

The views expressed in this book do not constitute legal advice. The laws and information covered within the book are correct at time of publication. The legal ideas discussed should never be used without first assessing your own situation and consulting a qualified solicitor. Neither the author nor the publisher can be held responsible for any issues encountered that may result from actions taken after reading this book.

To all those with a love of lifelong learning and who want to make a difference

To Tony and Charley, who had no idea I had a book in me and whose love and support allow my creativity to be channelled

Contents

Foreword

I vividly recall my first day as a property manager. A fresh-faced 19-year-old in the best suit I could afford from the proceeds of a Saturday job. I was soon convinced I had chosen the right profession. The job sold itself. Lettings and Property Management is a fascinating role and the many challenges it presents are part of its attraction; provided, of course, you are up to speed.

Back in 1995, nothing had prepared me for the journey I was about to embark upon. Induction and training were in their infancy, so it was a case of 'sink or swim'. I had to learn on the job and develop my own *modus operandi*, including the art of questioning – which happens to be one of the themes so well explained in this valuable text. I was enabled to cultivate this important art, and develop my knowledge of the business, by investing time interrogating experienced colleagues. Consequently, when I was promoted, I was confident in my ability to manage my own team whilst recognising I still had much to learn. It had become my responsibility to provide my team with accurate, timely and relevant advice. To that end I perfected my questioning style. Presenting the problem, considering alternative approaches presenting my preferred course of action and reviewing the received advice by further questioning. This approach has stood me in good stead throughout my career and has helped me navigate a host of complex legislative changes, whilst managing large property portfolios in the corporate arena.

Someone who has been subjected to my questioning style, and one of my principal advisers over the past twenty-seven years, is the author of this book. Gina Peters' expertise in our field is second to none. Her advice has helped maintain that balance between law and practice while retaining a commercial edge. *Lettings Law for Property Professionals* enables readers to tap into her extensive knowledge of the law as it applies to lettings and property management and receive advice on how to deal with numerous common (and not so common) issues that property professionals experience. Her advice on how to optimise one's questions encourages readers to critique their own questioning style. All of this is presented in a practical and interesting way, with a dash of humour for good measure.

How I wish such a text had been available to me at the start of my career but whether you are new to the industry or time-served, this is definitely a book property professionals must read.

Mark Chatterton, Group Lettings Operations Director, Connells Group

Introduction

Have you ever stopped to think about the way you ask a question and the effect that has on the outcome of your problem, both immediate and longer term? Not just the impact for you, but also for your colleagues and for building a more robust business. It's unlikely, as time is limited and the most stretched commodity.

My experience and knowledge are within the lettings industry and the law, and examples used are applicable to letting residential property in England and Wales. I have worked with many letting agents, both owners and employees, as well as those managing large residential property portfolios whether for or as a private or investment landlord or otherwise. The overarching aim for you as a property professional is to do your job quickly and legally, be the source of expert lettings knowledge and remain the consummate professional for your clients.

With about 175 pieces of primary legislation – and counting – to comply with to let a property legally, the lettings industry is not for the faint-hearted. The private rented sector is regularly at the centre of discussion, due to rising numbers of the population having to rent due to a lack of affordable housing stock. The younger generation are being priced out of buying a property of their own and are forced into the rental market. As a rookie specialist residential landlord and tenant solicitor in November 2001, little did I know how the demand for this niche area of legal advice would grow to such unprecedented levels.

As demand for private rented property has risen, so too has the number of landlords and letting agencies, not all of them with an appetite to raise standards within the industry. The emergence of the so-called 'rogue letting agent', and the even more malevolent 'rogue landlord', have been the catalyst for the deepening minefield of legal regulations and compliance in the sector. Unsurprisingly, property professionals have turned to legal advisors with a broader and firmer understanding and knowledge of the relevant legislation for fast and accurate advice on issues faced regularly in their jobs.

I recognise the pressures on property professionals and want to help you. Through using what I have learned answering questions over the years, I've written this book for those of you with a desire to improve not just your own knowledge and development within your profession, but who also want to use what you learn to improve the business you do. There is no need to be a member of a professional organisation or even have qualifications, though the industry may introduce such regulation. Being aware of the questions you are asking and making a concerted effort to regularly assess and act upon those answers when appropriate will support and help propel you forward in your efforts to improve and grow yourself and/or your business. Success can be achieved with a few simple steps which will lead to good retention of clients, improved reputation, larger client base and minimal disruption to commissions if this is your business. For over twenty years, I have run a highly successful lettings legal telephone helpline. Originally aimed at landlords and letting agents needing daily legal support, it quickly developed into a focused service for lettings professionals, and in 2015 it took on national status and expanded significantly to become a very popular membership benefit to members of Propertymark.[1]

I became a solicitor largely because the job sounded varied and interesting and supported my underlying desire to help people resolve a variety of legal problems. I secured my law degree from Exeter University, passed the Law Society Finals Exam and completed two years as a trainee solicitor before qualifying in October 1995. I loved litigation with

---

1   ARLA Propertymark, Facebook post (8 June 2018), https://en-gb. facebook.com/arla.uk/posts/the-legal-helpline-is-our-top-rated-member-benefit-log-in-to-the-members-area-to/2143062515711038, accessed 19 July 2022

its time constraints, discipline, tactical approach and vast array of legal issues to resolve. After six years I became a housing law specialist, full of reservations about whether I should be specialising to such an extent, and naively thinking I would run out of things to learn because it was 'too specialist'. How wrong I was. I love my work and am now a vested partner of a multi-disciplinary law firm and proud leader of a large and well-regarded landlord and tenant team.

It has been a tremendously rewarding journey and has, more recently, required much more of an educative and legal support role both internally for my team members but increasingly importantly for an incredible number of letting agents who put their trust in me and my team to guide them through the maze of legislation that they must apply to let property at the highest standard. I have presented legal updates face to face and remotely, and prepared and delivered both bespoke and standard training for clients and Propertymark respectively.

Using my considerable experience and knowledge of residential housing law I know first-hand exactly what you are missing in your telephone helpline questions. I also strongly suspect that you as callers won't know what to do with the answers you receive. Most legal questions are regarded in isolation, a unique question for that moment as you are intent upon getting the answer and cracking on with your work. You are potentially unaware that someone else in your business might have a similar, or even identical, lack of knowledge.

A knowledge gap can prove time-consuming in terms of finding a resolution. I have considered the key legal areas that generate the most frequently asked questions as you may not be aware of the regularity that these questions are asked. Designed to highlight the sticking points and allow you to realise you are not alone, this book will also provide you with a point of further reference until you can confidently apply the answers. I have developed an easy-to-apply method for asking the legal questions you need answers to when using a legal helpline. This is a simple process you can adopt to ensure you make the most of the time you spend asking, resulting in a positive return for you and/or your business.

Let me introduce the HOUSE rules which are a memorable process to work through before asking anything. HOUSE stands for Highlight, Optimise, Uncover (and Uphold) the law, Share and Evaluate. I explain and support each rule with real-life examples from my own experiences of being a lawyer and running a telephone helpline service. The rules are designed to help you avoid having to make repeat calls on the same issue and to help you as property professionals to become more effective and professional when working with your clients.

If the lettings industry does become regulated, it is even more important that you learn as much as possible about everything you undertake and use the knowledge wisely. This includes the way you ask legal questions to maximise return.

Simply follow the HOUSE rules and master the art of asking pertinent and effective legal questions in the broad and complicated area of lettings law. By doing so, you will lift your game, look great professionally in front of clients and reap the success you deserve.

PART ONE
LEGAL KNOWLEDGE GAPS REVEALED

The law contains an abundance of detail and is often drafted in a way which can put you off reading the legislation thoroughly. The answers are there, but it can take some unravelling and knowledge of everyday cases before real understanding starts to sink in.

Legal advisors are asked many questions daily. I have had my fair share over the years, stemming mainly from the increasing demands on you as property professionals to keep letting property legally compliant. The first part of this book looks at the most frequently asked questions and their answers, and introduces you to a memorable set of rules to apply to your legal questions to get the most from the answers you receive.

ONE

The Most Frequently Asked Questions In Lettings Law

What is it that everyone else asks about and does this align with your own areas for development? This first chapter is dedicated to looking at the legal topics at the heart of your most frequently asked questions. I highlight here the common areas that may perplex you, or give you cause to check what you are about to do. With a few examples and supportive explanations, you will have the answers you need to progress confidently and avoid the same questions in future.

Giving notice

One of the most important and essential tools in a property professional's armoury is knowing how to terminate a tenancy or licence agreement. Probably the single most important thing for a landlord investing in or letting a property is knowing that they can get their property back when they need to. Your job as the property professional in this regard is therefore critical. I suspect that this is the reason for the many questions relating to when to give notice, what notice to use, what notice period to give and expiry dates, how a break clause changes things and how best to serve the notice. Fear of getting it wrong coupled with a lack of confidence fuels the questions.

Let's look at three of the issues in the context of various tenancy agreements that shape the answers legal advisors give, as the type of tenancy is a big factor.

I start with the most widely used form of tenancy, the assured shorthold tenancy (AST). Section 21 of Housing Act 1988 as amended sets out the way in which notice can be given by a landlord to terminate an AST without any reason required. Form 6A is the form of this notice in England, though in Wales up until 1 December 2022 (having been postponed from 15 July 2022) industry templates were used for fixed term and periodic tenancies. The templates do not create that many questions, probably because they were also used in England until 1 October 2015, but Form 6A generates many regular questions.

QUESTION: I am not sure how to fill in Form 6A correctly. Does the landlord's name have to be on it at all? Do both the landlord and the agent sign the form?

ANSWER: The form is confusing as the initial version introduced in October 2015 did not provide space to put the information seemingly required for number 4, namely the landlord's name and address – a drafting error from the outset. This caused problems, as forms were served without any landlord details, not realising that they were supposed to be included as there was no obvious area for them. This resulted in awkward conversations with landlords explaining that the form had to be re-served. This was not a great situation professionally and resulted in possible further hardship for the landlord if rent was not being paid and meant a potential lack of commission for you. Now the form provides space for entering the landlord or landlord's agent details at number 4, but in my view, there is still a lack of space after the colon, and things remain unclear. You can complete the form without mentioning the landlord if you opt to put the agent's details here. This is also an issue as it means the landlord's name may not appear on the notice.

While it is not necessary as the risk seems to be removed with the use of the word 'or', one solution is for the name of the landlord to be inserted along with the agent's details, particularly if the landlord is sensitive about using their own address at this point.

Only you as the agent need to sign the form
which is comparable to me as an appointed
legal representative for my clients signing a
document. I too am an agent in this context.

Let me turn to non-Housing Act (NHA) tenancies,
otherwise known as common law tenancies, as these
seem to stump you, particularly the company let. A
common question is: What notice do I use to terminate a common law tenancy and when does it expire?

It seems simple enough, but common law tenancies do seem to create a mental block for some. As soon
as you veer out of the realm of the Housing Act 1988
where it feels safe, you are invariably subject to this
ancient alternative to statute-based law, the common
law, which is largely derived from judicial decisions.

A common law tenancy arises, or must be used,
when the annual rent exceeds £100,000 and/or when
the property is not the tenant's principal home. The
contract is not regulated by a particular law and in
many cases where the tenancy is not an AST it is a
common law tenancy. The tenant may be an individual or a company and in either case, save for company
lets during the fixed term, you must use a notice to
quit. The notice period is based on what is reasonable under the common law, which is a minimum
twenty-eight days. Generally, you follow the length of
the rental period as the measure for the notice length.
If the rent is paid monthly, you give at least a month's
notice. There is an industry-used template used for a
notice to quit, not a prescribed form but 'notes' or set
prescribed information in Section 5 of the Protection

from Eviction Act 1977 must be included on every such notice given. I believe that it is the wording on the template that gives rise to the problems:

> We on behalf of your landlord(s) [landlord(s) name] of [landlords address] hereby give you notice to quit and deliver up possession to us, of [insert property address] on [date] or the day on which a complete period of your tenancy expires next after the end of four weeks from the service of this notice.

The latter part is what is called a saving clause which means it ought to help you out if you do not get the expiry date exactly right.

Here's an example with a common law tenancy running month to month after the fixed term has expired. Rent is paid on the twenty-fifth of the month. Landlord wants to terminate. It is the sixteenth of the month now so using the wording above on the template notice you must make the notice at least one month in length and the expiry date must be at the end of a rental period. Notice given on the sixteenth of the month therefore terminates on the twenty-fourth of the following month to be valid, and you will still be able to factor in any service days.

Now here's a trickier example of a common law tenancy set up with rent paid yearly. Tenancy held over for the last two years without further fixed terms agreed. Landlord wants to terminate. The year began 1 June. It is 25 February. When does the notice expire?

This is more difficult because a notice to quit for a yearly tenancy which this is provides for a six-month notice period. Once you know this you must make it end, allowing for service, on 31 August, or 1 September because the period start date is the date of the year the tenancy commenced. The inclusion of the saving clause should help.

Remember, you do not need a notice at all to terminate a fixed term tenancy agreement of whatever type. If the tenant simply vacates at the end of the fixed term the contract is satisfied. To protect your landlord, you should serve notice to expire at the end of the term in case the tenant remains. This will save valuable time as your landlord can start court process immediately based on that notice if necessary.

I mentioned earlier that during a fixed term company let you do not need to use a notice to quit to terminate, you can use a simple letter, but the notice must be used if the company occupies beyond its fixed term. A company let always has individuals occupying the property with the permission of the company which cannot physically occupy anything itself, so invariably the template notice to quit is used, and particularly so if a break clause is relied upon. If the question relates to when the notice must expire using a break clause, you must read that clause carefully and follow it to the letter.

QUESTION: Can my landlord issue a claim for possession if the tenant retracts their notice to quit and decides not to leave, and the landlord has not served a statutory notice?

ANSWER: It is quite surprising how often this is asked, and it is a good question. When I first came across this years ago, I was certain the landlord would have to serve the correct notice and proceed on that basis as it seems far too weak to proceed on the tenant's notice. This is what happens in practice. However, there is authority[2] that once served a notice to quit cannot be retracted unless the party upon whom it was served consents to the withdrawal or waives the right to enforce it.

It is entirely possible for a landlord to base a claim on the tenant's notice, but I have not done this myself in practice and have not come across anyone trying it. As the notice to quit ends the tenancy and a new one starts, the landlord can claim double rent under an ancient statute, Distress for Rent Act 1737, and this may prompt a hasty departure by the tenant.

Breaches of tenancy and how to resolve

Another legal area that attracts a lot of questions relates to the use or interpretation of clauses within the tenancy agreement. My focus here is on the terms that cause most difficulty. I touch upon breach of a company let and use of the forfeiture clause later.

---

2   *Clarke v Grant* [1950] KB 104, Court of Appeal, www.iclr.co.uk/ document/1951000494/casereport_3130/html, accessed 7 July 2022

One of the biggest problems when you let a property is that it gives exclusive possession to the tenant. If you think about the general issue relating to gaining access, be that to fix something or if within the last two months of the tenancy to show prospective tenants around, you will all be able to recall tenants who made life as awkward as possible when it came to organising for you or a contractor to enter the property. Despite the fact that what you are trying to do involves making something work better or fix something that no longer works to improve the situation for the tenant, that sort of tenant is simply not interested. This sort of scenario can be frustrating and prove draining on your time, to the point where in some cases your landlord feels they have no option other than to remove the tenant. It may not be straightforward if the tenant is already shouting about disrepair items in the direction of the local environmental health officer, or you are at the start of a brand-new tenancy which means you are stuck until at least month five when you might get to serve a Section 21 notice. This type of breach by the tenant is common and difficult to overcome.

Other common questions concern pets, noise and nuisance, and sub-letting in tenancies. Pets have been a point of discussion in the lettings industry, to the extent that developers are now building properties purposely to allow tenants with pets to be considered. There is a lot of bad press about landlords not wanting pets in properties as they have convinced themselves that the property will be significantly damaged if they allow the tenant to have one. With more than four million private renters in the sector, and with the UK being regarded as a nation of pet-lovers, the issue is emotive.

With the introduction of the Tenant Fees Act 2019 and the limit on the level of deposit that can be taken for tenancies, landlords may consider asking for a higher rent to ensure they have some buffer for any excessive damage to the property. This is fine as long as you list the rent with and without a pet when you advertise the property. Otherwise, if the landlord refuses consent for a pet, the tenant may get one regardless. This latter point is what forms a common question.

> QUESTION: If the tenancy agreement does not allow for pets, and you know that the tenant has a cat in the property, or the tenancy only allows for one pet, and you know that the tenant has at least three dogs in the property, what can the landlord do?

> ANSWER: A breach of tenancy case such as this usually prompts you to write emails or letters to the tenant informing them that you know of the pet situation and that it is a breach of the relevant term of the tenancy agreement and that they must ensure that the pet is removed. How many tenants honestly do anything about it? It is as if they know how hard it is to do very much, let alone quickly.

You have the following options:

1. Allow it and terminate the agreement when the fixed term ends, or you can use any break clause if relevant if your landlord is annoyed or concerned.

2. Consider serving a Section 8 notice using Ground 12 for a breach of a term of the tenancy and giving the tenant the statutory two weeks to remedy the breach. When the pet is still there at the expiry of the notice revert to Option 1.

3. Serve the notice in Option 2 and then take an enormous risk by issuing a claim for possession based on the breach. I say this is a big risk as Ground 12 is a discretionary ground for possession and you are reliant on persuading a judge that it is reasonable to make an outright order for possession possibly far sooner than the tenancy is due to end. If the tenant turns up and admits they have two pets instead of one, but they seem a conscientious pet owner, you are unlikely to get an order. Your landlord will be out of pocket, in the same position as before and exasperated, so revert to Option 1.

There is a textbook answer for this – and I discuss when to apply these in Part Three. It can also apply to allowing access. However, to obtain a court order (an injunction) to force the tenant to do something is expensive, takes time and will feel like a sledgehammer to crack a nut. You may have little problem with the tenant and their pet ultimately. If there is severe damage at the end of the tenancy and costs vastly more than the deposit to put right, then the fall back is a claim for damages for those reasonable costs.

When it comes to noise and nuisance, there are standard clauses within most tenancy agreements requiring the tenant to treat the property in a 'tenant-like' manner, to keep the noise down in their general use of the property and not to cause a nuisance to anyone in the vicinity of the property. I have been involved in some nasty claims for possession based on Section 8 notices relying on Grounds 12 and 14, which is what these problems fall under.

The question usually is if you have received complaints from the property's neighbours saying that there is loud music all the time, that the tenant is rude and uses bad language in the communal areas of the building, that they think drug dealers are hanging round the property, that numerous men seem to be going in and out of the property which has several female occupants or other similar problems, how do you resolve? It depends on the severity and regularity of the incidents and, more importantly, nailing the witness evidence you need to persuade the court to stop what is going on.

Your landlord will have a much better chance in court, despite the discretionary nature of the claim, if you have witnesses who are prepared to support it. The witness needs to explain what it is that is happening and to what extent they are affected. However, will they turn up to court to give the evidence weight and credibility? Ideally, you want the problem to be ongoing and serious enough to guarantee a successful outcome for your landlord.

As soon as you mention a court appearance, however, suddenly your witnesses are extremely reluctant to take matters further. They often fear the repercussions of the tenant finding out who is testifying and worry about a hard time in the run up to the court hearing. In some drug cases the witness may fear for their own safety, and, even though they could call the police, it becomes virtually impossible to get them to help you. The police can be useful witnesses if they have been called out to deal with incidents at the property and will support such claims.

I have had cases where there are so many grumbling neighbours that those written complaints become the basis for the landlord or agent's evidence if witnesses prove difficult. There is no denying that if you end up with behavioural issues from a tenant a landlord may be forced to take court action which can be expensive due to lawyers charging by time taken to prepare. Thankfully, often such serious breaches are recognised as warranting an outright possession order. You must be prepared for the hassle and complaints that the landlord, or you on their behalf, will continue to receive possibly up to the point of the court hearing, which could be months away. You could try to negotiate to avoid the court process all together, by perhaps setting off rent to get possession amicably.

Finally, questions about sub-letting. The question usually is if you are sure that the tenant isn't living at the property and seems to have moved in numerous people when the property only has two bedrooms, or you looked through the lounge window and that looks like it is being used as a bedroom, what should you do?

This one I am sure will resonate with many of you, as it happens frequently and is difficult to control. Most tenancy agreements have a standard clause in them that prohibits parting with the property, be it wholly or in part, and this is what the tenant is usually in breach of if they have sub-let. There is good reason for this clause, as it keeps the landlord knowing who is in the property, particularly with duties of landlords to ensure that all adults eighteen years or over have the right to rent if the property is in England

The clause has been used with serious consequences for landlords in my experience, where the tenant has never intended to live in the property and then sub-lets immediately without the landlord's consent. You may have heard of 'rent to rent' where in contrast it is agreed from the outset that the tenant can sub-let, but this can quickly get out of control. Often the breaches relate to the sub-leasing clause being used in an underhand way. The local authority often becomes interested if there are lots of people using the property, as the property may then fall into the category of a House in Multiple Occupation (HMO), in which case where is the landlord's licence? An HMO brings with it more onerous regulations designed to keep its multiple occupants safe, but the landlord never intended for this scenario to arise. It could result in significant fines for not holding a licence and breaching the regulations. While you and your landlord are trying to resolve things, the tenant is creaming off a higher rent than was agreed originally and laughing at your expense.

These scenarios are messy and highly stressful for you and your landlords as they escalate fast. It is worth trying to get the local authority on board quickly to provide a temporary exemption for the requirement of a licence while you take court action against the original tenant to remove everyone. You should serve a Section 8 notice under Grounds 12 and 14, though in serious cases using Ground 14 solely will enable you to serve the notice and immediately issue the claim. I have not come across a landlord wanting his property to be something that it was never intended to be, and the time and money involved in this type of court case can be significant.

Death of a tenant

At some time in your career, you may be confronted by the death of a tenant. It may be through illness or natural causes, a tragic accident or as is sadly becoming more prevalent, suicide. I will also mention murder of a tenant as this can prove a little more problematic for you if the property becomes a police crime scene, but ultimately the same resolution unfolds as I will explain in this section.

Death is a difficult subject for most at the best of times. You will require a compassionate approach as a professional in dealing with next of kin in such circumstances. I hope to provide you here with the answers to the regularly asked question relating to the death of a tenant during a tenancy agreement.

The typical question is, if the sole tenant has died, what do I do now?

Answer: As you will appreciate, the law relating to death is one which as a solicitor you will have some general knowledge of, but it is a specialist area. I know sufficient about the basics associated with how to proceed with the tenancy but anything more complicated, such as paying inheritance tax or seeking a grant of probate and I would be checking the position with a colleague expert in the field. It is not a short answer and questions will follow from your legal advisor to try and establish what exactly you are facing as there are several scenarios on death.

The first and most important thing is that the tenancy does not simply end when a party to the agreement dies. It continues exactly as it was, and it is only the tenant's status which changes. You probably found out from someone that the tenant had died, and that person is the best starting place to establish a line of communication which you need with the next of kin. You originally took identification from the tenant, and you are now about to start dealing with that deceased's personal representatives, so identification becomes important at this stage. A personal representative is responsible for dealing with the estate of someone who has died. If that person is named in the Will, then that person is an Executor. If there is no Will then an Administrator is appointed – often being a family member. You must communicate quickly with the personal representatives, and you need to be sure that you are dealing with the right people. Do obtain identification for each person you are dealing with. A copy of the last Will confirming the appointment of the executor(s) is helpful with confirmation from a solicitor who may be involved, or an idea of the family line for intestacy (no Will) cases. There is a useful Intestacy Rules Chart that the government produces and is called 'Choice not Chance' (see Useful links page at the back of the book). The flow chart will help you ask the right questions as to who is likely to be a beneficiary of the deceased's estate.

Here are a few helpful tips on how to find next of kin:

- Start with putting the deceased tenant's name in Google. It might link to an obituary or a news article about the death or details of the funeral. This will provide some leads for you.

- Try and get a copy of the death certificate as this will state who registered the death and in what capacity. It may provide you with the starting point for the next of kin.

You can try an intestate search at www.gov.uk, which provides a list of unclaimed estates, though it may take a little while for this to start showing anything associated with a recently deceased tenant.

You can try a probate search (details can also be found at www.gov.uk), but if the death is within the last six months this will not be of use as it usually takes this amount of time to be registered.

There is a lot of good information at www.gov.uk including the details of the Official Solicitor and Public Trustee who can be emailed. If no one can be found, then the estate of the deceased will pass *bona vacantia* to the Crown, handled by the Treasury Solicitor, and there is a process for how this is done. This would be a worst-case scenario for you as a property professional as it can be time-consuming to ensure the removal of the deceased tenant's possessions.

Where a tenant dies, and you can find a good line of communication with next of kin, the initial conversations will need to be around removal of the deceased's possessions from the property. With possessions in the property, the contractual rent continues to be due, and the estate of the deceased is liable if it can support those payments. The landlord will need to be sympathetic to the situation, and I have known no further rent to be charged by the landlord after the death if the possessions can be removed quickly. From a practical perspective it is better that the tenancy is ended agreeably with the personal representatives so that a new tenancy can be organised as soon as possible to stop the pain of there being no rent paid for a much longer period.

In the situation where a tenant is murdered at or in the vicinity of the property, this will almost certainly result in the police wanting to cordon off the property as a crime scene. This scenario can take some time to work through and you should proceed to try and locate the next of kin, and the police will be able to support you with this. This will delay you being able to go into the property as well as any possessions being able to be touched. This could result in rent arrears accruing while the police finish their investigations at the property and even additional cleaning expenses for a professional clean, which hopefully the deceased's estate can pay.

The tenancy continues after the tenant's death, so the landlord is within their rights to seek payment for any rent outstanding until the property is finally vacated and cleared of possessions. The individuals you are communicating with are not personally liable as they are simply representing the estate of the deceased. The estate will hopefully have sufficient funds to meet the ongoing rent, but it is possible that there is nothing to pay your landlord with so the faster you can act the better. You must warn your landlord of this possibility from the outset.

The process can take months. If you find it difficult to locate any next of kin and you find yourself having to serve a statutory notice to terminate the tenancy you will need to refer to the tenant as 'The Personal Representatives of the Estate of the Late [tenant's name]' and serve it at the property. The Public Trustee will need to be served with a copy of the notice and there is a special form to do this. Be aware that there is a specific procedure to follow to ensure the tenancy is legally ended and this attracts a fee. It is better that a legal advisor supports you with this so that all possible outcomes are properly considered.

The tenant 'churn'

Another common question relates to a change of a named tenant where there are multiple sharers comprising 'the tenant'. Student lets and groups of professionals sharing accommodation as a joint tenancy tend to be the basis for the queries.

QUESTION: What's the easiest way to change one of the tenants in a multiple tenancy?

ANSWER: There are two ways to sort this out. A recent case, despite only being influential, helps us prepare for the way the judiciary are likely to think in relation to this issue. This is set out shortly as a case study. I deal with the question in the context of an AST.

A change of one tenant of several named tenants who are jointly and severally liable for all the tenancy terms amounts to a material change of the tenancy. Consequently, a change in any individually named tenant and the tenancy is effectively surrendered by the outgoing tenant and re-granted to the incoming tenant.

I have been asked by some agents whether they can use an addendum to the original tenancy to change a named tenant. You can, but this is unsatisfactory for several reasons:

- The incoming tenant starts their tenure from the point they occupy which will be different from any of the other remaining tenants.

- The inventory and check-in report will have reflected the property when the original tenancy began so how can this be dealt with fairly for an incoming tenant mid-term?

- How do you deal with the deposit?

- All documents must be re-served on the new tenant and all other tenants.

- Will everyone agree that the outgoing tenant can simply swap with someone?

By changing a tenant, you effectively start a new tenancy and that means all the above points must be sorted out. This will be a big effort on your part to resolve, particularly if you need the check-in report redoing. It will also require the landlord to meet the fees. I do understand why the addendum seems convenient and straightforward as it can be charged to a tenant as a variation of the tenancy, though only for the rather small fee of £50 inclusive of VAT. A brand-new tenancy is the textbook way to resolve a tenant 'churn'.

STURGISS & GUPTA V BODDY & OTHERS

Sturgiss & Gupta v Boddy & Others[3] 19 July 2021 – HHJ Luba QC demonstrated the danger of a landlord simply allowing tenants to change without any intervention from him at all. It is an appealed county court case but is likely to achieve some judicial influence in its interpretation as His Honour Judge Luba QC is an eminent Judge in housing law circles and has been at the centre of some newsworthy interpretations of regulations that have been of note (recall the gas safety problem relating to whether you must show that the tenant received the first gas safety certificate prior to moving in, thankfully now resolved).[4]

The landlord, Mr Boddy, entered an AST with four individuals as joint tenants in March 2004, before the compulsory deposit registration schemes were introduced. He took a deposit at the time and kept it safe throughout. He took a relaxed approach to any change in who the tenants were and allowed the tenants to sort out the deposit shares and changeovers themselves. There were three such tenant 'churns' shortly before Sturgiss and Gupta brought their claim against the landlord for compensation of between one

---

3   *Sturgiss & Gupta v Boddy & Others* [2021], Central London County Court, www.bailii.org/ew/cases/Misc/2021/10.html, accessed 7 July 2022

4   *Trecarrell House Limited v Patricia Rouncefield* [2020], EWCA Civ 760, www.judiciary.uk/wp-content/uploads/2020/06/Approved-judgment-Trecarrell-House-Ltd-v-Rouncefield-18-06-2020.pdf, accessed 7 July 2022

to three times the deposit for the landlord breaking the Housing Act 2004 Regulations relating to deposits.

The tenants argued that whenever a tenant changed it created a new tenancy and although the landlord did not deal with any change of tenant as if it was a new agreement, he effectively 'received' the deposit again at that point, which gave rise to the need for registration of the deposit and service of all associated documentation. None of this had happened in practice and the tenants alleged that there was a breach, and the penalty should be awarded to them for each 'churn'.

The judge's view was that there were ASTs in place, albeit periodic in nature, and that there had indeed been a material change in 'the tenant' whenever there was a 'churn'. He also accepted that each new cohort of tenants must be treated as having 'paid' the landlord the deposit again, every time there was a churn. Consequently, there were multiple breaches by the landlord of the deposit regulations as the deposit was not registered and had not been treated as needing to be at each churn.

The landlord was ordered to pay compensation to the tenants of one time the deposit for each 'churn'. It was regarded as at the low end of the landlord culpability for the penalty.

While generally prohibited unless with the consent of the landlord in ASTs, an assignment of the tenancy from the outgoing tenant to the incoming tenant may be the best alternative to regranting a tenancy on every churn. The incoming tenant takes on the liability of the outgoing tenant, with the consent of the landlord for the change, and picks up the tenancy from where the outgoing tenant left it.

If your landlord is willing you therefore create a deed of assignment. Good deeds should take the approach of involving all parties: the landlord to show their written consent to the change; the remaining tenants as they should agree to the change (as they will feel the greatest impact); and the outgoing and incoming tenants as they must agree. An indemnity is usually given by the incoming tenant to the outgoing tenant relating to all payment and obligations under the tenancy terms from and including the date of the assignment. Any deposit element of the outgoing tenant is met by the incoming tenant, and there is no further 'receipt' by the landlord.

While I like the deed of assignment, under the Tenant Fees Act 2019 it is regarded as a standard piece of work and you are only able to charge £50 inclusive of VAT as the permitted fee. With a good template the new arrangements can be documented and implemented relatively quickly. However, the landlord need not agree to a change in tenant and may not if the landlord must meet the additional costs associated with you undertaking the work to get this resolved.

Summary

This chapter has provided you with the most common 'hot' questions property professionals ask, their solutions and practical tips. The regularity of the questions suggests that the whole industry at times has problems in these legal areas:

- Knowing the type of agreement and how to give notice

- Breaches of tenancy and how to resolve

- What to do when a tenant dies

- How to deal with tenant 'churn'

TWO

The HOUSE Rules

The frequent questions that I have covered in the first chapter informed my creation of a method to support your daily business as property professionals involving legal lettings issues. You need to be able to find fast and reliable answers to your legal questions. While a telephone helpline service or a good accessible lawyer can provide this, my focus is on the questions themselves. What is it that is missing to enable you to appreciate the relevance and value of your questions in the business setting and to ensure that asking questions is a great use of your time?

My model provides you with five easy steps for asking better, more impactful legal questions, that will start making an immediate difference to you and your business. By using the HOUSE rules, you should consistently be able to see the results of taking regular action on the answers within your own work environment, including an increase in your personal self-confidence and easily maintaining your professionalism in front of your clients and colleagues.

What are the HOUSE rules?

Each letter of this fitting word forms the foundation for your journey to engage with legal issues as they arise. My primary aim for the HOUSE rules is to enable you to get the most from your time and improve your business with your questions. The rules are as follows:

- H is for Highlight

- O is for Optimise

- U is for Uncover

- S is for Share

- E is for Evaluate

I will explore each element of the model in Part Two.

The HOUSE rules allow you to prepare to ask your questions, and with very good reason, which will become apparent when using real-life examples. Asking questions is an art form. As the medieval philosopher Roger Bacon is attributed to saying, 'To ask the proper question is half of knowing.'[5] If you master asking an accurate question, then you are already on your way to knowing the answer.

The HOUSE rules are a mini checklist for your brain at the point you realise you need to ask a question, and, with perseverance, you will soon implement the method automatically.

The HOUSE mindset

Adopting the HOUSE mindset for asking questions is going to take some effort on your part. Any new habit takes on average sixty-six days before you do the new thing automatically.[6]

If you have work colleagues, you can form a supportive environment and remind one another about the rules. Put reminders by the phone or in the office somewhere regularly used, such as the kitchen or toilet, and try to use this approach before you pick up the phone with a query. You may find that you are pleasantly surprised at how smooth your call goes using the HOUSE rules.

Sloppy questions can lead to sloppy answers, or a vague question will take more questions from me as an advisor to get to the right question and ultimately

5   R Bacon, medieval philosopher, https://quotepark.com/
    quotes/1837308-roger-bacon-to-ask-the-proper-question-is-half-of-
    knowing, accessed 7 July 2022
6   P Lally, CHM van Jaarsveld, HWW Potts, and J Wardle, 'How are
    habits formed: Modelling habit formation in the real world', *European
    Journal of Social Psychology* (16 July 2009), https://doi.org/10.1002/
    ejsp.674, accessed 7 July 2022

right answers. It takes up more time, so the HOUSE rules provide you with the building blocks for forming your succinct question. Let's look at a real-life example to show you what I mean:

> CALLER: I've got this tenancy where the tenant is an absolute nightmare, they won't let us in to do any work, make excuses for not being in and are rude to everyone who tries speaking to them including everyone in the office. The landlord wants them out. What can we do?

> OBSERVATION: *The question comes eventually and the scene is set, but you will see from the reply and the series of questions that follow that it takes time to focus in on how to get to the answer.*

> REPLY: What sort of tenancy is in place?

> CALLER: It's a non-Housing Act tenancy.

> REPLY: Is the tenant an individual or a company tenant?

> CALLER: It's a company let and the people in the property are employees of the company. They are so difficult.

> OBSERVATION: *This has completely changed the basis for the answer.*

REPLY: Are you in a fixed term or is the contract now running month to month?

CALLER: They've only been in a few months.

REPLY: How long is the fixed term for, and do you have any break clause in the tenancy agreement?

CALLER: It was for… (*shuffling of paper in the background*) twelve months. Don't think there was a break clause… (*more shuffling*) No, no break clause.

REPLY: Do you have a forfeiture clause in the tenancy agreement, it's sometimes called a right of re-entry clause and usually lists what can happen if there are breaches of the tenancy agreement during the term?

CALLER: Forfeiture clause, not sure. Just a moment. Can't see anything. Oh, is this it (*reads from document*): 'If at any time the rent or any part of the rent shall remain unpaid for fourteen days after becoming payable (whether formally demanded or not); or if any agreement or obligation on the Tenant's part shall not be performed or observed… then the Landlord may re-enter upon the Premises…'

REPLY: Yes, that's a forfeiture clause. The only way to terminate the tenancy earlier than the fixed term agreed is to ensure that the behaviour you are describing fits in to the reasons for forfeiting the tenancy, so a breach of the tenant's obligations, but you need to find the clause they are breaching and be able to quote it. Are there rent arrears at all?

CALLER: Yes, the tenant hasn't paid the last two months.

REPLY: That may help you. If your landlord tried to forfeit with only the breach of obligations allowing access you may have trouble getting such an order to terminate the occupation early, but with rent arrears as well this may get worse if you leave it and is a stronger basis for forfeiture. You should serve a letter of forfeiture[7] setting out all the breaches and referring to relevant clauses in the tenancy. If the tenant remedies the breaches, which is always a risk, then you will not get anywhere with court proceedings. The stronger route is to evict on termination of the tenancy, but you are a little way off the end of the term at this stage so you can at least send a letter of

---

7   6 A letter of forfeiture does not have a prescribed form and should clearly set out the forfeiture clause, the breach, and the time limit in which the tenant should put the breach right or you will take court proceedings. You must serve it at the property and at the company's registered office.

forfeiture and see how it is received. Happy to help further if you need it.

As you can see, the legal advisor has had to ask six questions of their own to get to the right answer to the original question. Some legal areas are admittedly much more involved than others, but the more information that you have at the outset and the clearer you can be with your facts, the easier and faster it will be to resolve the question.

When broken down into its five parts, the HOUSE rules may at first seem onerous, but the relevance of the word will bring it to mind instantly, and you will find you can deal more easily and quickly with legal issues. Regard HOUSE as the foundation for all your future legal concerns and build on it.

The impact of ignoring the HOUSE rules

I would not have written this book if I did not think that with a few simple changes to your mindset about legal questions you will be able to achieve much more than just the right answer. This may be the first time that you have properly considered what your legal questions are like. I am not here to impose a solution, merely to give you the tools to work with should you choose to do so. It's easy to understand, and you have nothing to lose and everything to gain by giving it a try.

As I see it at present, when you encounter a legal problem, various scenarios arise:

- There is no one to talk with about the issue.
- You have a pretty good idea of the answer but want a confidence boost to confirm your judgment.
- You are not sure what the answer is and need help.
- You don't know what you don't know.

The latter is the most frightening, but if you ask, you should be OK and will learn over time. If you keep up with regular legal updates you have access to and industry insights, you will become familiar with what is going on at least in the private rented sector generally. This should provide you with sufficient knowledge about relevant lettings issues to get you thinking there is something more to know about certain issues when they arise. While you may know that there are numerous pieces of primary and secondary legislation that comprise lettings law, sometimes the application of it to a practical situation makes it feel difficult and creates doubt.

A huge further increase in legislation governing the lettings industry in both England and Wales is predicted, and some big changes have been planned and talked about within various White Papers and consultations. So, you need to be proactive now. You may consider that the various qualifications that you have under your belt are enough, and a certain level of qualification may become compulsory if the Regulation of Property Agents (ROPA) is introduced. Lifting your knowledge out of the textbook or exam paper and putting it into practice is the key to succeeding in business. For instance, it was not until I got into an office that I started understanding how to be a lawyer and applying the textbooks to the problems my clients were telling me about.

My role as a legal advisor is becoming more educative than ever, but the questions people ask are the fun part as they reveal the real value to the legislation in question and could even result in amendments being required. In a lawyer's world it is the testing of the statues against real-life situations that brings the law to life, and it all starts with legal questions about everyday scenarios that do not appear to fit the legislation. A Court of Appeal or Supreme Court case is what most lawyers dream of getting involved in, as these important and influential judicial decisions create the precedents that shape the legal field.

STREET V MOUNTFORD

The case of *Street v Mountford* [1985] UKHL 4[8] is an older case in point and is still relied on and underpins the basis of a tenancy agreement. The House of Lords has now been replaced by the Supreme Court so the

---

8   Street v Mountford [1985] House of Lords Judgment, www.bailii. org/uk/cases/UKHL/1985/4.html, accessed 7 July 2022

judgment in this case was from the highest court in the land at that time.

The story is simple in that Mr Street had granted Mrs Mountford the right to occupy rooms five and six in his property at 5 St Clements Gardens in Boscombe for a rent of £37 per week by an agreement which stated it was a licence.

The question to be decided by the court was whether the agreement was a licence as stated or whether what had been granted was a tenancy. The terms of the licence included that Mr Street could enter the rooms at any time to inspect, to read the meter, to carry out maintenance or for any other reasonable purpose. Only Mrs Mountford could occupy and sleep in the room. The licence could be terminated on fourteen days written notice, and it expressly stated that the licence did not and was not intended to be a tenancy, so there was no protection at that time from the Rent Act 1977.

The court held that the agreement was in fact a tenancy. Lord Templeman's decision concluded that 'there is no doubt that the traditional distinction between a tenancy and a licence of land lay in the grant of land for a term at a rent with exclusive possession'.

The fact that Mr Street did not attend the property or provide services to the property were indicators to the court that the arrangement was a tenancy. It is all about whether the agreement satisfies all the requirements of a tenancy in which case it will be a tenancy. It doesn't matter what the parties think they have created if the effect is that of a tenancy.

I have used this case given its primary position in lettings to help clarify what any agreement might actually mean. Some tenancy agreements purport to be a company let but clearly started out as an AST with incorrect Housing Act 1988 references. You must know what you are doing from the outset to avoid confusion and poorly drafted legal documentation, which could affect your landlord in regaining possession.

It is fundamental to know your starting point. It is difficult in some cases to work out what exactly the parties have created; however, for most tenancies granted to individuals, an AST is the most common given the presumption in legislation from 28 February 1997. The definition of assured tenancies is found within Section 1 of the Housing Act 1988. This section sets out that an assured tenancy is a tenancy under which a dwelling-house is let as a separate dwelling so long as the tenant is (1) an individual, (2) occupied as the tenant's principal home and (3) not a tenancy that is excluded under the Act from being an assured tenancy. It is vital to check this whenever you create an agreement to ensure it is correct from the outset.

If you are unable to improve the accuracy of the questions you are asking and ensure others in your immediate work environment are aware of anything that you learn to improve their working habits, then the ability to service all property professionals in the lettings industry is seriously compromised. To save time, ensure that one question properly resolves your legal issue as fast as possible and brings the confidence you need to ensure your clients are serviced at the highest level. The impact of not using the HOUSE rules is most obvious when speed is of the essence, which for all of us nowadays, is most of the time.

Legal helpline

Now that you understand the basics of HOUSE rules and how they can help you as a property professional dealing with lettings law, I can explore the value that your questions can generate.

There are many ways in which you can find answers to your legal questions. You may know a good lawyer to call, have internal legal counsel or have access to a legal telephone helpline linked to a law firm, an insurance policy or a specific industry membership benefits package. A helpline is great, as it generally provides a fast fix, but it is useful to realise the potential they provide including those who get asked the questions. Given the number of legal questions that arise, why not make them count? The choice is yours. You can continue to ask questions such as the following.

> CALLER: I've served a Section 21 notice, but the tenant hasn't vacated and is now saying they aren't moving as the notice is wrong. I cannot see anything wrong with the notice, can you help me as the landlord wants the tenant out?

REPLY: Can I just check that you have an assured shorthold tenancy agreement – when did the tenant move in?

CALLER: Oh goodness, I inherited this one, and they've been in years.

REPLY: OK, I need to know exactly when they moved in. Do you have that information please?

CALLER: Let me just see (*frantic paper shuffling*). It's not obvious but there is a tenancy here that goes back to 1994.

REPLY: Does that tenancy agreement state anywhere that it is intended to be an AST?

CALLER: Yes, almost at the top it says exactly that. So it must be, right?

REPLY: On the face of that agreement yes, but because the tenancy was started after the Housing Act 1988 began on 15 January 1989 but before 28 February 1997 you need to let me know if you have the Section 20 notice that must go with it to make it an AST.

CALLER: Not sure what a Section 20 notice is. Can't see anything like that on the file, no. No, it doesn't look like there is one, but the

AST says it's one. Then there is another AST agreement dated 2000 and that's it.

REPLY: This is likely why the tenant is saying that your notice is wrong. Without that Section 20 notice you cannot treat the tenancy as an AST, and it reverts to being an assured tenancy. This means the Section 21 notice is not available to your landlord to remove this tenant and they must rely on Section 8 of the Housing Act 1988 and the grounds set out in Schedule 2. This type of tenancy gives the tenant more security and unless you can prove one of the grounds the tenant can remain in the property.

CALLER: You mean the landlord cannot get this tenant out? They want to sell.

REPLY: You must either find the Section 20 notice or prove one of the seventeen grounds, as I said.

This is another example where the tenancy type is fundamental to getting the right answer, but it takes six questions in response to the first question to get to the real problem. It will probably have taken ten minutes minimum to get to the bottom of the question, and the caller will still have needed guidance as to what to do next to save face with the landlord. The landlord will not be interested in the fact a key document is missing; instead, they will be alarmed by the resultant change in security for this tenant which will hurt them badly if they cannot remove the tenant fast. If they put their trust in you as a property professional to set up the tenancy then regardless of whether you or another firm have lost documents, or have not done something, it will now be you picking up the pieces.

So how could this question have been asked well? Presuming that you know the issues with tenancies that predate 28 February 1997 but started after the Housing Act 1988 began, you can start asking questions like the following call.

CALLER: I am concerned that I may not have the right documents to prove that what looks like an AST is one as it started in 1994 and I cannot find the Section 20 notice that I need to confirm the status. The landlord would like me to serve notice but while we have always treated the tenant as one with an AST, I know we are in trouble without that notice.

Can I just check with you whether there is anything I can do as the tenant is not in rent arrears and is a good tenant, so I don't think we have the grounds for a Section 8 notice at this time?

REPLY: You are right, you may be in some difficulty unless you can locate the Section 20 notice. See if the local authority has a copy if they have had any involvement from the outset, ask the tenant (possibly risky as it may raise an eyebrow as to why), or even the landlord. If this is not possible, then you need to explain the problem to the landlord. Good tenants are hard to find, but if the landlord wants them out, they may have to invite a surrender and negotiate it. However, it is worth seeing what reaction a Section 21 notice if served has as it may result in the tenant leaving without a problem, or it will flush out whether they know their position without the Section 20 notice. I wouldn't advise that you issue a claim for possession based on it though for the reasons we have discussed.

The second version of this question is from someone who clearly knows what they are talking about, so it is possible to explore what sort of steps to try carrying out in view of the key issue – the missing Section 20 notice. Business growth from such a question is plain to see as the answer leads to further practical knowledge and time was well spent in calling to ask the question. It could even help to avoid a big issue with the landlord.

Asking good and informed questions is about building on and retaining good business relationships with your clients. It's about remaining knowledgeable, reliable and trustworthy which will improve your confidence even when the situation is not quite what you had hoped for and is not necessarily down to any action of yours. By tightening up your questions, you will receive faster and more purposeful answers, leading to better business decisions.

Summary

This chapter introduced the HOUSE rules, and throughout the book I will give you more examples and great tips to start making those legal questions work for you.

I have provided some reasons to start thinking about using this model for your legal questions, not least:

- To provide you with a focus and clarity to your questions

- To reduce the time you spend asking

- To make the time you spend asking valuable

- To realise the importance of knowing what your question is based on

- To get the most out of what you put in

- To gain confidence and practical solutions from your questions

- To realise the business growth potential behind great questions

PART TWO
A GUIDED TOUR OF THE HOUSE RULES

The HOUSE rules form the transformational basis for your legal questions. By exploring the questions that are regularly asked you'll find that many property professionals have the same type of issues.

This part of the book shows how you'll gain more from your legal questions using the HOUSE rules. I explain each element of the HOUSE model in turn, allowing you to connect with and understand the five key areas of focus – Highlight, Optimise, Uncover, Share and Evaluate – which, with regular use, will transform the quality of your questions to benefit your business.

THREE
Highlight The Problem

If you do not raise those everyday problems as they arise you end up with a much bigger and more daunting problem, as the situation is either left unsolved or escalates. There will always be the one file or one client that you tend to want to steer clear of or do not enjoy working on or with, but unless these are tackled head on, there can be serious consequences. So, first you need to highlight the problem. This is a great starting point and can help you to develop on both a personal and business level.

The starting point

One definition of the verb 'to highlight'[9] is to draw special attention to, and this is what I am talking about here. This means highlighting the legal problem that has arisen, whether that is mentioning it in conversation to someone, deliberately making time to discuss it with someone depending on the perceived complexity or taking a neon-coloured pen and literally highlighting the area that you are not understanding. This flags the issue to be further thought about, but you'll need to do something about it promptly to avoid further stressing and delay.

You should feel comfortable raising any legal question and be positively encouraged to draw attention to or highlight any issue that you may have, be it big or small, legal, or otherwise, as it will make your life a lot easier if you can feel comfortable talking to someone about it. For instance, a legal telephone helpline is a great, fast solution to many legal questions, and yet it may be acting as a crutch if not carefully managed and considered for the more junior property professional, or one who works alone more than most. What I want to raise attention to here is the need to create an environment where there is a real haven for all property professionals, at whatever stage of their career, to ask whatever they need to.

---

9   'Highlight', *Oxford Learner's Dictionaries*, www.
    oxfordlearnersdictionaries.com/definition/english/highlight,
    accessed 7 July 2022

The first step is not, therefore, to simply pick up the telephone and call a legal advisor. That will give you the answer, but you may miss the opportunity of getting a great example of where the issue arose previously and was applied in practice. You cannot beat a good relevant story for committing it to memory for future use. That is why it is important to start within your team.

Each of your colleagues will all have different levels of knowledge. It is essential that wherever you are working you feel able to highlight those legal issues and get them out in the open. You can then see whether it is something that as a team, however small that may be, you can resolve because someone has come across it before, or that you have highlighted something which has been overcome through a process that you did not know about.

I am not trying to put you off asking questions, quite the opposite. The questions should arise freely, but you should only highlight and commit to asking a legal advisor those questions where the legal issue has been exhausted among your own thinking and peers initially. Many of you already do this but sometimes you may find that everyone is out or unavailable and you have something to sort. If you have no obvious supervision then a helpline is a fantastic tool never to be under-estimated, and you will not be judged for whatever you are asking about.

To highlight a legal issue is an essential first step in obtaining a great solution but try and get the knowledge flowing among your own peers before taking it to an external source for the answer. It is likely to be much more satisfying, memorable and possibly more relevant to you.

Factors holding you back

For some, questions might seem like an obvious and unwelcome legal knowledge gap, a hurdle to be overcome in the most discreet way possible. For others, it's a natural part of learning. I can alleviate any barrier you may be putting up relating to the extent of your personal knowledge and understanding, as everyone processes and learns in different ways, but it is easy to compare yourself to others who may, frankly, seem like they know everything.

Whichever camp you fall into it does not matter as there is no absolute right answer and it is down to competing factors in your personal life. Everyone is unique and will work with questions in different ways. My objective is to help you recognise the blocks you create and for you to realise the importance of asking readily. I am going to highlight where you as an individual may have a problem with asking the question in the first place. If you know this, and I can provide some reassurance and shed some light on some of your own self-perpetuating messages to yourself about asking, you will be in a much better position to feel confident that you can, and should, ask.

I suspect that one or more of the following may resonate:

- My question is so simple I cannot possibly ask it because I feel stupid, or everyone will think I am.

- I just keep getting stuck on the same legal problem and despite asking can't seem to remember the answer or apply it. I feel useless.

- What will my colleagues / manager think of me if I ask that?

- I should know this.

- I know there is something not right here, but it will show someone up if I raise it.

I can honestly say I have been through all the above scenarios at one time or another in my career. I am not usually the one asking what sounds like such a brilliant question at a seminar or lecture, and I have sat there asking myself how on earth that person thought of such a great question and why I can't think of anything to say. So, in this scenario you must ask yourself:

- Who is telling me that it's a great question and that I can't come up with one?

- Why am I beating myself up as I haven't got any questions?

- Why am I wondering what everyone would think if I did ask a question?

You will not be surprised to hear that it's enemy number one talking as usual – your own inner, and usually negative, self-talk. This has a great deal to do with how you deal with a given situation and can hold you back. The worst form of this is when you magnify the negative aspects of a situation and filter out the positive ones. It is a difficult mindset to get out of, and everyone does it to varying degrees. Some people can rewrite that script, but others will get stuck.

Using a telephone helpline as a tool to gain your answers is, by its very name, designed to help you. The primary aim of the person on the other end of the telephone is to give you the right answer fast and let you get on with your day. You become confident, the service is excellent in your view and it is a positive experience. This book is here to help enhance the process of asking a legal question for you as a property professional and get even more out of it than you may be at the moment. It most certainly is not to make you feel anything other than positive about your newly acquired knowledge.

You will recall that at the start of this book I revealed several legal topics that questions are most often asked about. For some of you they may be easy, but I bet you can understand why those questions are being asked, and that if you were starting out now you would be glad to know there are a lot of others with similar knowledge gaps. It just helps ease that element of self-doubt and that fact alone should be a comfort.

What you should also appreciate is that legal advisors with a telephone helpline service to operate are not there to judge anyone calling. Legal advisors answer the question to the best of their ability and in an easily comprehensible way. I have learned from and trained many helpline legal advisors and legal professionals, and guess what? They have the same negative inner self-talk as I have highlighted for you in answering the questions *What if I don't know the answer, what if I don't understand the question, what if, what if, what if...?* A helpline is a massive learning curve for those taking your calls and at various times the person answering may be a lot more nervous than you are asking the question, but they will get you the answer.

In all the years I have been operating a helpline service, there is rarely a question asked that a legal advisor may not have the immediate answer to, but it does happen and that's where the fun begins as advisors try and work out what that answer is and get back to the caller. This is improving the advisor's knowledge too.

The positives of asking

Questions are a valuable indicator of an inquisitive mind. They demonstrate your engagement with what you are doing and keep your mind active. Questions may prevent you from getting on at that moment if your knowledge and understanding does not extend far enough, and what you do next with the questions is important.

I have already explained that sharing the burden of a question is a positive step as it immediately brings others into helping potentially or at least pointing you in the right direction. This, together with getting over the possibility that you are in some way reticent about asking the question at all, are great positive actions.

Asking is effectively highlighting the question or issue that has arisen and as no one is expecting you to know everything, you should adopt a positive mind-set and ask. In fact, you should feel free to ask as many questions as you need to, whether that is within the confines of your work environment, to a legal advisor or through a legal helpline. The latter will likely have a fair usage policy, but provided you are polite, you should be able to ask questions whenever, and however many times, you need to. You probably will not get through to the same person for each call, and, in any event, you are not being judged for the quality of your question. The only thing to watch here is whether you are getting enough support in your work environment if you find yourself constantly having to rely on a third party for your answers. Positive activity within the workplace using questions can be so productive and listening to others ask and respond is another great way to see positive development within a team of property professionals. If you enjoy and feel safe in the workplace, you will naturally ask more.

For me, the most significant positive from asking a question is that it is satisfying to get an answer which helps you understand the problem fully and enables you to get a letter written, a contract out or a better process mastered. There is nothing I like more than solving something for a colleague or a client. If you work on how you interact and support your clients, for those more junior among you, you may find yourself getting noticed. I cannot think of anything more positive than asking questions if it results in kudos.

From the perspective of a legal advisor, a practical solution for you is the best result in a lot of cases for your questions, and this is illustrated later. Another great attribute of asking questions is that it shows that you are keen to learn and have an active brain, particularly if within your workplace. I encourage everyone I work with to keep asking questions, as it is far better that the questions get asked than not, and I am about to explore why.

As you gain more experience you should find that your questions become quite slick and are less frequent, but this will take a while, so one positive step is to consider enrolling on an industry course to start obtaining a few qualifications. If you do, and many have if they are members of large trade bodies for property professionals as it is almost expected, you will gain personal confidence. Just to have a basic knowledge and understanding and share good practice with others who are on such courses will provide excellent building blocks for further, more sophisticated, legal questions that will inevitably arise in the future.

Many see the expected introduction of the ROPA as a positive step for property professionals. This will provide for an independent property agent regulator who will operate and enforce compliance of a single mandatory and legally enforceable Code of Practice for everyone in the property industry. This will undoubtedly help improve the standard and status of letting agents and other property professionals.

There are very few, if any, legal questions that are not positive in the complex labyrinth of lettings legislation that lurks to trip up the unwary. Questions by their nature are designed to explore, examine, delve deeper into a subject, unravel, and ultimately create positive outcomes for those that are bold enough to ask. Why wouldn't you?

The personal consequences of not seeking help

I do not wish to cause unnecessary alarm in the next couple of chapters as they highlight the consequences of not seeking help with your questions and learning gaps when you need it – both for you personally and for business potentially. However, it sometimes helps to understand fully why it is important that you keep asking.

For example, when I was about a year into my job as a newly qualified solicitor, I remember that the absenteeism of one of the junior personal injury paralegals was getting more and more apparent, not just to that person's immediate work colleagues but across the firm. It reached a point one evening when it transpired that their supervisor had decided to look in the employee's room to see if everything seemed OK, and discovered a plastic bag tucked away under the desk with a large pile of unanswered post in it dating back months. Clearly something had been wrong for some time. I forget now how many matters had to be reported to insurers based on the firm's negligence for missing a deadline or a limitation period for issuing a claim, but it hurt the firm. I do not believe that person set foot in the office again and lost their job, unsurprisingly.

There are questions to be asked in this scenario and lessons to be learned from both an employer and employee perspective. For instance, how was the problem not picked up so much earlier? Where were the checks or supervision support for the employee? Why did the employee feel they could not ask and get the right level of support for the workload? Were they overloaded? And so on.

You would think that an incident like this could be spotted easily, but I was caught out some years ago when an employee did almost the same thing. They started being absent and making excuses for things which did not seem right. Recalling the earlier incident, I looked through a few desk drawers and I was glad I did. I uncovered numerous sheets of paper needing to be filed, invoices not sent and letters not appearing to have been dealt with. It was nothing like the scale of the earlier example, but it started to make sense when I realised what the person had been hiding and why they might be struggling to come in and face the team each day. This situation similarly ended with the person leaving of their own volition. I generally regard myself as a good judge of character, but I didn't see this one coming. No one is infallible.

I appreciate that these examples could have the most dramatic impact on you personally if you do not ask for support or guidance at the right time – you lose your job. I am directing this to those who are employed and perhaps in more junior positions where such situations can easily become serious quickly.

You may be feeling more secure as the owner of a business, but I am sure that even you need someone to bounce ideas off, get a second opinion from or obtain a legal answer on occasion. I know I do, partner or not. More to the point, if you as the owner get it wrong the personal embarrassment factor hits harder in terms of reputation, and that can easily extend to the business generally. Whatever role as a property professional you find yourself in, be it senior or more junior, you should always know where to turn for support should you need it.

I have mentioned the factors which can hold you back and start you on the slippery slope of feeling like you can't get help. It is vital to work within an environment which suits you best and brings out your natural curiosity to know more and be able to ask what you want when you want without repercussions. I would rather have numerous questions every day from my team than very few, or worse none, and therefore not know where someone is on their legal journey. It is worrying for supervisors and difficult to manage.

One of the more obvious consequences of bottling things up and not asking legal questions is stress. High anxiety and stress are two of the most common ailments to manage at varying levels in your life. Stress and anxiety do not emanate solely from the workplace, but why fuel it by not asking legal questions as they arise? It is easier said than done I know, but however trivial to you, a legal issue has the potential to evolve into something that has major impact if not dealt with fast.

For example, imagine you are an enthusiastic new lettings coordinator at a reputable firm, and you meet with a new landlord who has ten properties and who asks you to organise a company let on one of those as soon as possible. The company let is a type of tenancy you haven't come across before. It can't be that different from a 'normal AST' though, can it? You want to make a good impression in the office so you can't possibly (you think) reveal that this is not something you know anything about. You start sorting it out based on an AST. As you work through having sourced your company tenant there seems to be a lot that doesn't make sense, but if you chop and change a few parts it works. You get the tenancy signed up to for two years without a break clause, and the company tenant has occupied for a few months when they stop paying their rent. The landlord wants something done and after the usual letters you boldly confirm that you will serve a notice on the tenant and put together a Section

8 notice based on the usual rent arrears grounds that you are familiar with.

It would be interesting to know how many of you are cringing right now, possibly understanding the problem as you may have experienced it as a new starter in lettings, and may be wishing you had had a helpline to support you way back when. This still happens where an AST has been turned into a company let and it is not pretty. What happens next?

On the day the notice expires, with no rent paid, the tenant company via their licensee occupant director emails the office to say that the notice is invalid. It is picked up by your manager as you are not in the office, and the problems start to unravel in your absence as your manager is forced to look at the file more carefully.

The basics relating to tenancy type are critical in setting up a tenancy agreement and can result in the need to check and ask a few questions, even if just to make sure. This scenario could easily play out badly, leaving you to be called in to your manager's office when you are next in, only to face resolving this not just for you but for the landlord. It will leave you feeling humiliated, small, and most of all wishing you had asked as soon as you knew you had never done such a let before. It just isn't worth the fallout. A good manager will of course take you through what a company let should look like and help you get everything back on track. Remember from *Street v Mountford* that you cannot call an agreement a licence if it is a tenancy and the same goes for an AST if it's a company let, nor can you treat it as such. The bigger headache would arise if there were no forfeiture clause within the tenancy agreement as you have a two-year fixed term without a break. This will leave you without a remedy before the end of the two years as well as a lot of rent arrears that the landlord might start looking to you to cover in view of your poor tenancy drafting. Usually, an AST has one included despite the landlord needing to obtain a court order for possession to remove the tenant so there ought to be this option available in this company let example and you can then serve a letter of forfeiture. With any tenancy of twelve months or more you should ask whether a break clause is required to alleviate problems such as nonpayment of rent at an early stage of the tenancy.

Try not to regard your questions as failings but as steps for learning. Covering things up will never help and will lose you respect quickly. It may lead to you not being able to gain a promotion, losing the trust of your colleagues and, at worst, losing your job. Mistakes that can be easily avoided with a quick question can be the costliest to you personally, so there is no excuse not to ask.

The business consequences of not seeking help

In this fast-paced and social media-driven world it is easy to let a lot of people know instantly that you are not their favourite company to work with. Unhappy customers in particular will use every channel available if something is wrong with a product or service to voice their negativity. There are great things happening on social media, but when it comes to the darker side, it can mean significant problems to your business, potentially beyond your control. In an ideal world there would be no need to fear making a mistake, but humans will go out of their way to make you and their friends aware of an error or a poor service or experience. This is what you as a business are up against in a world where everyone is 'too busy' but is quite ready and able to complain fast.

Setting expectations from the outset for everyone working in a business can eliminate those moments where you may feel like there is no one to turn to or ask, be that from internal sources or an external one. It is better to ask those legal questions before you do something wrong than to start unpicking the problem created by a mistake or misunderstanding.

'Remember that time is money' is an aphorism that was originally intended to relate to the monetary cost of laziness in the workplace, but it also illustrates the monetary cost to a business of not asking questions before you carry out something that you are not sure about. As a property professional your landlords are often busy individuals who are looking for a good return on investment or regular income from the property you let and/or manage. Without solid legal knowledge to work from you can easily make a very expensive mistake for your business.

Let's highlight one such example. You need to ensure a valid notice is served. Here are two scenarios:

(A) The landlord is coming back from the United States after working out there for a while and wants their property back to live in. They want you to serve notice on their tenant so that they can move back in.

AST now running periodic, no problem you say (and hopefully mention that if the tenant does not move out then legal process will have to be taken which can take months). You serve a Form 6A Section 21 notice and all the prescribed documents are all re-served just to be sure. The notice expires the day before the landlord has said they are back – two months away and that seems to work.

You pop the notice through the door on your way home from work at 6.30pm on a Friday night. Job done. 14 January delivered and 15 March expiry (leave an extra day as taught).

The tenant starts messing around with rent payments for the two months' notice period and won't let anyone in for access to do anything, viewings or otherwise. They make it clear just before the notice ends that they are not going anywhere on 15 March.

You are left with the landlord arriving in the UK in two days, some rent arrears and did you spot

the other problem? Yes, the notice will be deemed
served at best on Monday 17 January, so your
notice period is short on being at least two months
in length. The notice is invalid.

(B) The same scenario above can be applied to a
landlord wanting to sell and finding a buyer but
only based on vacant possession. The same facts
occur but the purchaser pulls out due to your
invalid notice and the extra time that it will take to
get the tenant out.

Until you get very well acquainted with serving
notices and tenancy agreement provisions you may be
unaware of certain key things that must be complied
with to get the notice served validly and in line with
your expiry date. Deemed service is one such area
and you need to be very confident with it to make the
necessary allowances when calculating your notice
periods and check the tenancy agreement carefully
for this.

In Example A, the landlord is not just going to
have to find somewhere else to live for a good while
but is facing loss of rent (unless insured) and a further
two-month delay to get a valid notice served before
the court process can be started. The court claim alone
can take a long time.

You may have had to deal with something like this
for a landlord and it cannot be easy. You must set the
landlord's expectation of getting their property back
right at the outset as there is always a chance that

the tenant will not vacate. If you tell them upfront the worst-case scenario, you can at least say that you warned them. If they don't have insurance, then the rent arrears are going to hurt both the business and the landlord, and not only where your commissions are based on receipt of rent. All of this will be a problem before you even face tackling the invalid notice.

In Example B, you are going to have to also contend with the possible reduction in the purchase price ultimately of the property due to the delay with the notice and tenant not vacating. In this scenario, I would suggest that you put your insurers on notice at this point just to be safe.

It all comes back to my starting point that 'time is money':

- If the tenant delays and does not pay rent, it impacts the business and the landlord.

- If the property professional gets the notice wrong, then it creates a further two-month delay and impacts the business and the landlord.

You must deal with this scenario very quickly if you hope to avoid the landlord losing faith in you as a business and possibly tweeting or posting their annoyance for others to see. Once it is out there, the damage is done.

It is worth me mentioning at this point that there are some hefty penalties lurking among various key areas of lettings legislation that could greatly impact the running of your business if you are found in breach. These are the important ones to be aware of (England only):

Immigration Act 2014 and 2016 – right to rent breaches

Penalty – five years' imprisonment or unlimited fine for renting property in England to someone who you know or had 'reasonable cause to believe' did not have the right to rent in the UK

Housing Act 2004 – HMO licensing regulations

Penalty – prosecution and unlimited fines, but rent repayment orders and management orders are also possible

Housing and Planning Act 2016 – provisions to prevent unlawful eviction or harassment, HMO licensing breaches, seeking a prohibited payment, among others

Penalty – banning orders to prevent landlords and agents from letting or managing residential properties

Housing Act 2004 – deposit regulations

Penalty – one to three times the deposit (if you as the property professional for your landlord get this wrong you will have to reimburse your landlord) and at worst multiple times

There are plenty of others and some are particularly easy to fall foul of. The financial penalties are designed to hurt but are aimed at 'rogue' agents or landlords and not those trying to make an honest living from a lettings business. It is, however, easy to trip up and miss something unless you have procedures in place to support everyone working in the business. This includes the ability to get a strong legal answer to your questions when you need them. I would recommend that you be sure to ask as soon as an issue emerges.

Summary

When you first come across a legal knowledge gap, highlight that question. Remember that:

- Getting the problem shared with someone else can help no end

- Being bold and overcoming that inner voice which tries to put you off due to pride or embarrassment is worth it

- No one is judging you as much as you are, so get over it and say something

- It's great to help your colleagues and clients, and it builds your confidence when you act upon the answer you obtained

- The personal impact of guessing or thinking you know can seriously set you back in your career and is stressful

- The business impact of guessing or thinking you know can be devastating and could hike your insurance premium without good negotiation skills

- Bad news travels fast

FOUR
<u>O</u>ptimise The Question

You have got that legal issue ready to resolve and you know who to ask about it, but now to follow a process to minimise your time getting that answer and maximise the benefit of it. The word 'optimise' means 'to make something as good as it can be; to use something in the best possible way'.[10] This fits the purpose behind this next chapter exactly, helping you to get the most from the question you ask.

Busy lives often lead to quick fixes, but there are problems ahead if you go tearing through to a legal advisor, spew out the problem in a garbled way, think you've got the answer, apply it and then realise it isn't the question you meant to ask. Using examples, I will

---

10 'Optimise', *Oxford Learner's Dictionaries*, www. oxfordlearnersdictionaries.com/definition/english/optimize, accessed 8 July 2022

show you why in fact it can be critical for you to ask the right question and optimise your legal questions.

The importance of asking the right question

You might think that surely when you contact a legal advisor you know what you want to ask, and this must be the most basic part of calling. Unfortunately, this is not always the case, as I have discovered over the years, and it can lead to prolonged questioning of the caller to establish what exactly the question is.

Take this following example of a call:

> CALLER: I served a Section 21 notice to terminate an AST, but the tenant didn't vacate so the landlord issued proceedings. The claim got thrown out as the tenant was represented by the Duty Housing Solicitor, and they said that I had not served the right edition of the *How to Rent Guide*. I can't understand what I have done as it was served at the start of the tenancy, and I gave the landlord the evidence. Can you help?
>
> REPLY: Yes, I can. (*Which could be the simple answer, but it doesn't really help.*) When did your AST start?

CALLER: 3 February 2020, so I served the edition of the *How to Rent Guide* dated 7 August 2019. I don't know what's happened.

REPLY: That seems right, so when did the fixed term end?

CALLER: It was a twelve-month term, so 2 February 2021.

REPLY: What date did you serve the Section 21 notice?

CALLER: 6 June 2021.

REPLY: Did you serve any further edition of the *How to Rent Guide*?

CALLER: No, was I meant to?

REPLY: Only if there was a new edition produced during the tenancy and the tenancy has now gone periodic or was renewed. This would amount to a replacement tenancy.

CALLER: There hasn't been a renewal, the AST is just running periodic.

REPLY: The latest version of the *How to Rent Guide* was released on 10 December 2020 which was during your tenancy, so at the point it went periodic on 3 February 2021 a new edition was available and that edition should have been served to ensure a valid Section 21 notice could be served. Therefore, the Section 21 notice was deemed invalid.

CALLER: What's the law that this falls under please as I have missed this somehow?

REPLY: The Assured Shorthold Tenancy Notices and Prescribed Requirements (England) Regulations 2015 – Regulation 3.

CALLER: I still don't understand why the court couldn't just make an order based on the Section 8 notice as there were rent arrears.

REPLY: What Section 8 notice? (*First time the caller has mentioned it.*)

CALLER: Well, the tenant was in three months' rent arrears, so we served a Section 8 not long after the Section 21 notice.

REPLY: Was that used in the possession claim as well?

CALLER: Yes, but it was still thrown out – the landlord used both notices.

REPLY: Well, that should have saved the day if the Section 21 notice was invalid. What grounds did you use?

CALLER: Ground 8 – the tenant owed three months' rent initially, but by the time the claim was heard it was down to just under two months of arrears.

REPLY: You say Ground 8, any other grounds in the notice?

CALLER: No, just Ground 8.

REPLY: The claim failed because the tenant reduced the arrears to below two months owing by the time the court heard the claim. If you didn't have Grounds 10 and 11, or even just one of those discretionary grounds included in the notice, unfortunately the judge cannot make an order as you have not made out the one ground you relied on in the notice.

Whenever I have taken a question on why something went wrong it can take a lot to unravel the history of what exactly happened. This example is no exception but as you can see, the question is not right from the outset. The caller has led us down the path to thinking that their Section 21 notice is the problem, but that is only half the story. No wonder the landlord isn't happy. Would you be if you had served not one, but two notices that did not get the order you wanted? It is unfortunate with the Section 8 notice not using all possible rent arrears Grounds 8, 10 and 11, as you must cover all your bases. You cannot afford the tenant any wiggle room, or, as in this case, you will end up with an angry landlord seeking compensation for taking a claim which was only going to succeed if the tenant hadn't paid off some of the arrears. There is nowhere to go as you did not do your job properly.

Often, as with this example, the caller must be asked a series of more specific questions to get to the real problem. It can be quite a task, and sometimes all the paperwork must be gone through while asking before the real issue is revealed. It's also time-consuming and you can end up feeling that the caller needs a lot of support with their learning. Other than offering to do the job for them, which of course legal advisors can, they are going to have to get some help when they put the phone down.

This next scenario I remember doing when I was a trainee solicitor needing some help. You walk in with one problem but end up with a bigger one which unravels as you talk, rather than explaining the serious problem right at the start. For you, it's like walking into your line manager's office with a file and asking this sort of question:

> QUESTION: I've not managed many flats in blocks before, and we have a flat in a block that we are getting complaints from the manager about saying the tenant is being too noisy as

they have parties late at night and play music very loudly. I've said we will have a word, but we have already done that a few times. I think we need to serve a notice, so which one do I serve?

ANSWER: Sounds like nuisance to me, have you got written complaints from neighbours or just the manager?

QUESTION: Just the manager.

ANSWER: Is this an AST?

QUESTION: Yes.

ANSWER: Section 8 notice then using Grounds 12 and 14 should do the trick, but you need plenty of ongoing problems to be confident of a positive outcome in court.

QUESTION: OK. There also seem to be a lot of people in the property all the time, and we have an email from the local authority suggesting we now have an HMO and what are we doing about it. They mention needing a licence and possible overcrowding.

ANSWER: So just a minute, this is serious. This isn't just about nuisance. This is much more serious for the landlord. Have you spoken to them?

QUESTION: No, as I wasn't sure what to do.

ANSWER: Well, now I know what's happened, we'd better look into this fully, and I'll guide you.

This scenario works well here for optimising the question and is also one that I explored in detail in Chapter One as a frequently asked question. This type of poor questioning is down to a lack of experience and a need to get better at asking the right question from the outset in a short and concise way. It can be tricky to know what is most important if you haven't dealt with such a problem before, but there are better ways of preparing to ask and optimising that question. I will give you some pointers, but first let's turn to look at the impact if you don't explain all the facts to a legal advisor.

The critical need to explain all the facts

If you do not provide all the facts for the legal issue that has arisen, you may get the right answer for those facts but the wrong answer for your question. While a helpline call is likely to be recorded, other direct calls to legal advisors are unlikely to be, so in the latter case it is even more important.

The first National Assembly in Wales was elected in May 1999. The Assembly represents the interests of Wales and its people, makes laws for Wales in specialist areas of daily life, agrees certain taxes and holds the Welsh Government to account. With a population of about 3.2 million, about 5% of the population of England, Wales has chosen in many areas to veer away from what the English Parliament is deciding. This means that as solicitors practising in both England and Wales, my firm needs to keep up with the differences in lettings law to be able to advise those property professionals among you who practise solely from Wales, or those whose businesses hold portfolios that include property that is situated in Wales, accurately.

I mention this as I remember a call from a property professional who was asking me enthusiastically about which type of notice to use to terminate a tenancy and to be honest it all sounded straightforward, so I was confident that I had given the caller the right advice. Suddenly, she let slip that they as an agency could produce their licence, and I was immediately alert to the fact that she might be in Wales, and I had given her completely the wrong advice as the caller and property were based in Wales. If only I had known that from the outset as this fact made such a critical difference to my answer. I kicked myself for not asking, but where you as property professionals know that one fact could change the entire legal advice given, please give it at the outset of your question. As there are relatively few property professionals in Wales compared to England it can be something not initially checked when someone seeks legal advice.

Just to confirm why my answer was suddenly wrong:

- A Rent Smart Wales licence has been a legal requirement for those letting or managing residential property in Wales since 23 November 2015. There is no equivalent in England, which is why it rang alarm bells when it was mentioned.

- Form 6A does not apply in Wales, and the rules associated with Welsh Section 21 notices are different.

The Welsh factor is a missed element which impacts on legal advice, so I would urge that you mention that the property is in Wales at the start if there is the slightest chance of receiving English advice from the person you are speaking with.

Another example would be useful at this point so that you can start to appreciate where questions go wrong in the broader sense without critical facts. This is not uncommon as there is some useful legal knowledge that is generally not properly understood which creates the issue.

Here is an example scenario:

CALLER: I've got a problem in one of our properties with trespassers. I haven't got a clue who is in the property, but it's not the tenant.

Can you help get these trespassers out please? What do I do?

REPLY: How many people are we talking about?

CALLER: It seems like three adults and two children, and we don't know their names other than one is called Marcus, or how they got there.

REPLY: When you say the tenant is not there, was there a tenancy that you organised at this property?

CALLER: Yes, my company found two tenants just over two years ago, and the AST has been periodic for just over a year now. We haven't been told by either tenant that they've left, and the landlord is worried as there seem to be more people in there and I don't know who they are. They must be trespassing.

REPLY: Can I just check, are you receiving the rent and if so, who is paying it?

CALLER: The tenants are still paying the rent, sometimes late but they are not in arrears. There is a completely new family in there, though.

REPLY: It doesn't sound as though they are trespassers.

CALLER: They must be as the landlord didn't allow them in.

REPLY: Your tenants must have though, and rather than trespassers they are therefore likely to be sub-letting from the original joint tenants and have been permitted to be in the property. Not trespassers, but a breach of tenancy terms almost certainly if the landlord has not given any consent for the tenant to sub-let.

This example swings from the caller thinking I am dealing with trespassers to – with some useful questioning from the legal advisor – a breach of an original tenancy agreement for sub-letting. The next question is, 'How do we get them out though?', and the answer lies in acting against the original tenants whose last known address is the property. You could instruct an enquiry agent to trace the tenants and serve a Section 21 notice on the property and new address, but it might take a Section 8 notice under discretionary Ground 12 if you were tied up in a fixed term still.

With this question the caller has concluded that the help needed relates to trespassers, but this is entirely wrong, and it is only after a mention of the occupiers 'not being the tenant' that the right pertinent facts can be drawn out. It takes time to sort out and if you can avoid it try not to pre-empt the solution as it could, as in this case, be different to your initial thoughts.

There are a lot of questions that start out as one legal issue and end up as a different one, generally because all the information at the outset is incomplete and missing those critical facts to lead immediately to the right answer. This leads conveniently into some guidance for you in how to prepare your question.

Tips for preparing your question

There is often a better way to do the things you do regularly, but because you are so familiar with them, you just do them almost on autopilot. Asking a question is in the same category, and unless someone mentions a different, more effective way to consider asking one, then you will continue to do as you do, and this is a key purpose of this book.

I was amazed, on further investigation, that the subject of questions is documented and discussed by many authors and is regarded, in literary circles at least, as 'an art form'. I am not intending to make you think about your questions in as much depth, but it did make me realise that this part of the HOUSE rules, to optimise your questions, is likely to be a sufficient prompt for you to focus on what exactly you are asking and how.

Benjamin Franklin in 1790 is credited with saying, 'If you fail to plan, you are planning to fail.'[11] This res-

---

11   B Franklin, 'Advice to a Young Tradesman', *The American Instructor: or Young Man's Best Companion* (21 July 1748), https://founders. archives.gov/documents/Franklin/01-03-02-0130, accessed 7 July 2022

onates with me as there is strong truth in this adage. You may regard it as somewhat dramatic a quote at this point, but is it? You can take it into all areas of your business and personal life wherever and whenever you need to prepare for something. Preparing your legal questions will make a tremendous difference to getting right answers.

Here are my tips, based on my own experience, to help you optimise your questions. Whether you need to ask a work colleague or a legal advisor, there is a strong case for you giving some of your questions more thought than perhaps you do before asking them.

Some questions are straightforward, so provided they are specific there is no problem. For example:

- QUESTION: What does this clause mean in the tenancy agreement? ANSWER: You read it out.

- QUESTION: How often do I have to obtain an Electrical Installation Condition Report (EICR)? ANSWER: Every five years.

- QUESTION: Do I need a new Energy Performance Certificate (EPC) to serve a Section 21 notice if the current one has run out? ANSWER: No, provided the original was served on the tenant, and you have not had a material change or renewal of the tenancy agreement.

- QUESTION: Is it possible for one of the joint tenants in a periodic AST to give notice to terminate for just that tenant? ANSWER: Yes, one tenant can terminate their liability during a periodic tenancy.

You get the idea. However, whenever you need to explain the context of the problem before you get to the crux of your legal knowledge gap which you need the legal advisor to understand and help you with, you will need to consider the following three tips for successfully optimising your question and securing an accurate answer. I will take each in turn and provide you with some examples, which are in no way intended to be exhaustive as there are many possible questions:

1. Ensure you have all the pertinent facts to hand and know the purpose of your call. For example:

   - If you are asking about a tenancy type or want to serve a notice you should be able to recite when the tenancy began – both the very first tenancy and the current one if renewed.

   - Know the type of tenancy, though if you are asking for help to know which type of tenancy dates become more important as does content in some cases, so have a copy of the tenancy ready.

   - Know where you are in the tenancy – fixed term or periodic – and if there is a break clause if the former.

- If you are asking about breach of tenancy not linked to rent, be able to explain when it started and exactly what you know about it and how. With company let breaches, you need to be able to confirm if there is a forfeiture clause if you are in the fixed term, so keep the tenancy to hand as you call.

- Are you wanting to confirm which notice you should use and in what form or are you wanting help with the completion of the notice?

- If there is a major water leak at a flat that you manage, do you want to know whether the tenant should be held liable or is the leak from another property into the one you manage?

- In all cases where you are instructed to serve notice, what are your landlord's intentions – to get possession, or to give the tenant a chance if they can sort out a breach?

- Only ask an essential question and keep it simple. Questions can easily turn into a long back-and-forth of numerous questions from both sides as the conversation progresses if you are not well prepared. In some cases, I appreciate it can be difficult to know where to begin, but if you can pinpoint the real crux of the matter and relay that to the person you are speaking to at the start, it can immediately narrow the possibilities. Explain what you need to know as simply as possible. For example:

- I am struggling with the expiry date of a Section 21(4) (a) notice for a periodic tenancy in Wales. The rental period is monthly from the thirtieth of each month, but the expiry date will be at the end of February and that month doesn't have thirty days. What do I do? You make the expiry date in March which does have the right number of days.

- I served a Section 21 notice last week but have suddenly realised that we only got the EICR through for the property a few weeks ago. Is this a problem to the validity of the Section 21 notice? No, the EICR is needed but not required to ensure the validity of a Section 21 notice.

2. Listen to the full answer to your question and don't interrupt. While this is self-explanatory, what I should highlight is that if a legal advisor, or a work colleague, has listened to the facts of your problem, you should give them the courtesy of listening to the explanation of how their answer is reached. From experience, there is nothing worse than being interrupted mid-flow as this can throw you off your train of thought and make it difficult to get things back on track, especially if more facts are added or changed. Conversations on loudspeaker with more than one person on the call can be particularly problematic if multiple people are speaking at once, or there are interruptions from others in the room. You should be polite and listen and try to give thorough and

correct facts from the outset to avoid alterations which may then affect the advice to be given.

Clear and concise leads to the right advice

As property professionals, you are likely to be out during the working day and a legal question may arise while you are on the move. The strength of your mobile signal can play havoc with how clear your question is relayed, as can the noise in the immediate area. This tends to extend the length of any call due to repetition while you intermittently cut out, but also makes it very difficult for the answer to be given confidently.

With time being so in demand, your questions need to be as clear as possible and concise. You must try and avoid rambling, give pertinent background as needed, stick to the key facts ideally in a logical order and get your question asked as soon as possible. If you have prepared the question, then this should all be obvious and will fall into place. You will get your answer quickly and be provided with a clear route to progress through the problem that you presented.

Sometimes you may seek help when you think you already know the answer. Let's call it a confidence boost. However, as with the following example, sometimes a poor question can be a huge time drain for both you and a legal advisor. Two things happen:

1. You state the question in a way which will support what you want to hear as the answer.

2. You do not get the answer you were expecting and consequently ask again, this time with some additional or possibly a few different facts. This can easily lead into a third time of asking if you are still not entirely satisfied with the answer.

Take this scenario which is from a real question that was asked:

> CALLER: We want to terminate an assured tenancy and want some help ensuring we use the right notice.

> REPLY: Unless you have a breach of tenancy and a ground made out under Schedule 2 of the Housing Act 1988 you cannot terminate it.

> CALLER: OK. That's thrown me a bit, so I need a Section 8 notice.

> End of conversation.

Now take this scenario with the same caller:

> CALLER: We tried to terminate an assured tenancy with a Section 21 notice and got caught out as the tenants took advice and told us we couldn't use that notice to end the tenancy.

REPLY: Can I check when your tenancy began?

CALLER: 1994. It was set up as an AST, but we simply cannot find the Section 20 notice, so we think that is enough for the tenant to treat the tenancy like an assured tenancy. Is that right?

REPLY: Yes. Does the tenant know you haven't got the Section 20 notice though?

CALLER: I don't know, but they did seem to take advice as we served a Section 21 notice, and they said it was invalid as the tenancy was assured.

REPLY: It sounds as though the Section 20 notice is missing, and you will have to treat the tenancy as assured which means proving a ground under Schedule 2 of the Housing Act using a Section 8 notice.

CALLER: They haven't paid rent for over four months.

REPLY: That is your answer then. You can serve a Section 8 notice on Grounds 8, 10 and 11, but if the rent is reduced or paid then you will not be able to get an outright order or possibly any order. You don't have any choice though as Section 21 is not available.

The two calls are different in terms of useful content, and it took a couple of attempts to get to the bottom of it. You need to be careful with the terminology associated with assured tenancies because this is the umbrella title and includes an AST within its definition (see Chapter Two for explanation). The caller knew that it made a difference not to have a Section 20 notice to hand but did not mention this until the second call. The use of 'assured' tenancy in the first call determined the answer quickly, but not as the caller had been expecting. As you can see, the second call is quite different in terms of detail given and made it easy to give the right legal answer knowing the facts supporting it.

It may be helpful to have a few examples of well structured, clear and concise questions, so here they are with a mixture of legal topics:

QUESTION 1: Can you please confirm when I need to use a deed for a tenancy agreement and why?

ANSWER 1: Section 52(1) of the Law of Property Act 1925 provides that an interest in land must with some exceptions be made by deed or some formal writing. However, Section 54(2) provides that leases of not more than three years do not have to be by deed. Some tenancy agreements seek a witness for the signatures even if they are under three years in length, but this is to prevent denial later that the person signed it.

QUESTION 2: Please can you confirm when I need to serve a new edition of the *How to Rent Guide* to make sure the Section 21 notice I need to serve is valid?

ANSWER 2: You must ensure that the guide is served on the tenant when a new or replacement tenancy is given to a tenant. You serve the guide that is current at the time of that tenancy commencing. If the guide is updated, then you should serve a copy of the updated guide at the start of any subsequent tenancy. This includes statutory periodic tenancies. As there is no penalty for serving the guide late, currently it is often served again if it has been updated prior to a Section 21 notice being served as a belt and braces approach, but it must be the edition that should have been served at the time the new or replacement tenancy was given, not simply the most recent.

QUESTION 3: I am preparing a tenancy agreement for six joint tenants, but I seem to recall that only four tenants can hold the legal title. Is this right and what happens to the other two?

ANSWER 3: You should put all six tenants on the tenancy as they can all be pursued in contract for any rent or other contractual liability under the tenancy. It is true that the legal ownership of the property under the tenancy will be held by the first four named tenants on trust for themselves plus the other two. This happens without any mention of it in the tenancy agreement. This is as much as you need to know.

I hope that from these examples you can see how concise the questions are and how from such questions a precise and accurate answer can be provided.

Summary

To get the best from your legal questions you must Optimise them, and this requires thinking before you ask. You need to ensure that you:

- Ask the right question
- Explain all the facts
- Prepare for the question you want to ask and keep it simple
- Ask only essential questions
- Don't ramble
- Keep the question clear and concise

FIVE

Uncover And Uphold The Law

To uncover – or to establish what legislation, if any, applies – and uphold the law is precisely what a lawyer does for their clients. As property professionals, you also do this for your landlords. It is at the centre of the HOUSE rules and the key to unlocking those legal issues where you cannot see how to apply the law to the situation you have, or there is a gap in knowledge of the law that requires support. It can be the most difficult element, but you are not alone. There is always help available, and you need to be bold and go and seek it.

In this section, I take you through the common thread running behind many legal questions, the reasons behind why it exists and the reassurance that it can be overcome. I discuss some of the trickier parts of lettings law and those areas where there may be a few surprises for some.

What your questions reveal

There are predominantly three categories of questions that property professionals ask:

1. Those emanating from the tenancy.
2. Those specific to legislation, be that primary or secondary.
3. Your 'live' scenarios that you require practical advice with.

These are the obvious ones and do not comprise an exhaustive list, notably those questions that relate back to your terms of business and to certain court processes. It is the tenancy questions that I am focused on.

Property professionals have in the past struggled to promote their work as a serious profession. This has changed hugely over the years, particularly with the evolving and now prominent large trade bodies representing many within the lettings industry. With ROPA perhaps closer to formal implementation, gone are the days when the lettings profession is held in anything but high regard, though the odd rogue agency rears its head to tar the brush a little. Formal qualifications will further enhance the value that you as property professionals demonstrate daily and give the public even more confidence in using you to help them through the ever-growing and regularly changing array of relevant lettings law.

The big difference between the legal profession and property professionals is regulation. You cannot simply set yourself up as a law firm, not for some years after qualifying. You can set yourself up as a letting agent or similar property firm without any recognised qualification or affiliation to any trade body and without any regulation, save for a few areas of law requiring certain memberships – client money protection and being a member of a recognised property Ombudsman to name a couple. This may be an indicator as to why one of the most asked about subjects is the tenancy, such as the type of tenancy / agreement, interpretation of clauses, drafting of clauses, execution of the tenancy both timing of and how, legal or equitable, how to terminate or surrender, how to change the tenancy, reliance on tenancy terms including unfair terms, parol tenancies (in writing or oral but not by deed), succession rights and impact of death of parties, to name a good few.

This reveals even more about the questions you ask as the tenancy (or whichever type of agreement is used) is at the heart of lettings. It is the single legal document that binds both landlord and tenant in the letting of all types of property within the private rented sector and is the document of greatest legal importance.

If you study law whether at entry level, degree or any other level of legal qualification there is one common thread running through so many subject areas and that is always studied to some extent – the law of contract. This is a vast subject which compromises critical knowledge for the lawyer in whatever field of law they may specialise in. It is of no fault of yours as a property professional that you enter lettings ready to learn the profession 'on the job', and so miss a critical layer of legal knowledge relating to contract law.

I have always considered that a good grounding in this area of law is essential to properly understand why tenancies are set up and work as they do. This is key for why you need the most support with the contract that you negotiate between landlord and tenant and guarantors. There is no judgment associated with this, it is a fact; therefore, it is not surprising that most legal issues arise from the tenancy. You can get to know why things happen as they do by experiencing them, but the deeper knowledge will only come and a better and longer-lasting understanding created if you study contract law to some degree. If you get the chance to explore the subject within training accessible to you as a property professional, I recommend it.

The same can also be said of your own terms of business, which is another important document. Like a written tenancy agreement, this sets out the basis of a contract between you and your landlords. Questions arise regularly about terms of business, particularly when something goes wrong, and should be referred to if the landlord considers that you may not have done something or acted beyond what you were instructed to do. There is more than breach of contract at play as the tort of negligence may be involved as well as the law of agency, and I touch on the latter and its effect shortly. I've provided here plenty of examples to show you what I mean about contract knowledge gaps and the reasons why behind the answers.

Basic knowledge gaps within contract law

This section is not designed to be a mini lecture on Contract law. What I want to illustrate are two areas which give rise to the most questions and then explain the contractual principles that support the answers.

The first question relates to the contract's formation, or at what point you have a binding agreement. This becomes most important in cases where one of the parties decides to withdraw before the tenancy starts.

Take the following scenario: You negotiate a tenancy agreement with a tenant on behalf of your landlord on the fourth of the month. Everything is sorted – including references – and the tenancy is due to commence on the eighth. The tenant signs the agreement on the fifth, and you have authority to sign off on behalf of the landlord, but you don't immediately do this. The payment of the first month's rent and the deposit is due on the day the tenancy commences. On the seventh, the landlord changes their mind and wants to withdraw from the tenancy before it starts. Is there a binding tenancy or can the landlord walk away?

You need to recognise the basic principles of contract law to <u>u</u>ncover the answer. The scenario necessitates a look at when the contract is regarded as formed. Be aware that you can have a verbal contract (ie, a contract not in writing), but in this example the tenancy is in writing, though only the tenant has signed. You can even have a contract based on the conduct of the parties or an oral contract and whichever it is, the same contract rules will apply.

Looking more closely at the example, you need to work out whether the five essential components of a contract are evident:

1. **An offer**: The landlord made the offer of the tenancy through you as their agent.

2. **Acceptance of the offer**: The tenant has accepted the offer as they have signed.

3. **Consideration for the agreement**: Consideration is required by each party to the other. This can be a promise to pay money, so the tenant's consideration is the rent and the landlord's promise is to let the property to the tenant.

4. **An intention to be legally bound**: Each party intends to be legally bound by the contract. In this case, there is formality and there has been the offer and acceptance required.

5. **Each party has contractual capacity**: Both parties are individuals of at least eighteen years of age, so they are legal entities recognised by law.

In this case, the tenant is relying quite properly on you as the agent to sign off on behalf of the landlord once they have accepted the terms of the tenancy by signing it. You have no reason not to sign, other than the landlord the day before the tenancy commences saying that they want to withdraw. This would be a breach of contract as all elements for a properly concluded contract are there, despite your physical non-signing at this point. This does not provide the landlord with a legal remedy not to proceed with the tenancy as the intention to conclude the tenancy was there from the outset and the tenant relied on that.

You would have to warn your landlord that if they failed to give the property over to the tenant on the agreed commencement date, they would be in breach of contract which would have the potential to result in a significant claim for damages for all associated losses to the tenant. This could be linked to moving costs, emergency stay elsewhere as your landlord fails to hand over the keys as the tenant has given notice and had to move out of their property, plus any other reasonable and foreseeable costs that have arisen from the cancellation of the tenancy for the tenant. Not a pleasant situation to be placed in as a property professional.

The second issue that you often ask about relates to guarantors for tenants. There are several ways to bind a guarantor be that an agreement included within the tenancy, a separate agreement of guarantee or a deed of guarantee. Let me take you through these, as they all seem to be regularly used within the lettings industry without any one taking precedence.

AN AGREEMENT FOR GUARANTEE

Be this a stand-alone agreement or incorporated into the tenancy agreement, it needs to be treated carefully and the order of signing becomes crucial to ensuring that good consideration is given by the guarantor. Using an agreement automatically means you are subject to contractual rules and all five components must again be there.

The tricky part is knowing what the consideration for the guarantee is. It is not obvious with a guarantor who is not paying anything or doing anything. The consideration is in fact the act of the landlord granting the tenancy to the tenant. The order of signing the tenancy is important to ensure that the guarantee binds the guarantor. You must arrange for the guarantor to sign first, and this is because 'past consideration' is no consideration, and the guarantor could challenge the validity of the contractual guarantee successfully if they can show they signed later than other parties. This can now easily be shown through e-signing. Signatures can be evidenced with the time of signature, particularly as with a contract there is no need for the document to be witnessed.

A DEED OF GUARANTEE

If the tenancy predates the guarantee, then the guarantee must be executed as a deed. This is a document stating that it is intended to be a deed and signed by the guarantor and witnessed when signed. With a deed it does not matter when it is entered into relative to the tenancy being agreed because no consideration is required for them to be valid. Deeds are distinctive to contracts.

This is useful in multiple sharer tenancies as it can get confusing when there are also multiple guarantors. To add to this, a student let, for example, can be signed months in advance of the tenancy's start date, so the set-up becomes even more important as students do not tend to have any income stream and the guarantors are vital. Get the guarantees wrong and the landlord will not have that essential back up for payment of the rent and other liability under the tenancy and that could prove expensive – for you.

To conclude, you need to be mindful that to be effective the guarantee needs to include useful terms to support the ongoing liability of the guarantor, despite continuation or extension of the original tenancy. There are various ways to do this, but over the years I have seen several terms within agreements for guarantee that have rendered the guarantee effectively unenforceable for being unfair, or others being an express restriction on the overall liability of the guarantor. This may not have been intended but is there.

The problem arises as landlords try and protect themselves from a tenant who may have weaker references because either they have been living abroad pre-tenancy, or their income is too low to obtain a 'pass' and a guarantor is required.

The main areas to watch out for in guarantee agreements, as they are subject (after 1 October 2015)[12] to Part 2 of the Consumer Rights Act 2015 and unfair contract terms, are:

- Only providing liability for unpaid rent and not damages for breach of any terms of the tenancy as well

- Limiting the liability to the existing tenancy only and not any form of continuation with perhaps a new tenant

- Not capturing a rent increase for the guarantor because the original tenancy did not contain a rent review clause and link the liability to rent payable 'under the tenancy' or something similar

- Allowing the tenancy to roll into a statutory periodic tenancy which, unless the tenancy provides for contractual continuation, does not then allow for rental increases so any rent review clause in the original tenancy is irrelevant

- Providing for liability for 'any variation or extension' to the tenancy, as this may end up

---

12 Prior to 1 October 2015, The Unfair Terms in Consumer Contracts Regulations 1999 provided the basis for unfair contract terms.

being unenforceable as the guarantor may be regarded as having to pay way over what they originally signed up for, causing the guarantor to be liable for rent increases

If correctly drafted, the only element of the guarantee that will drop out is the unenforceable term, everything else should remain in place.

Due to these variables, you should carefully check that your guarantee covers what you want it to and what you are instructed to provide for your landlord. If in doubt, you may need to re-execute the guarantee at the point of renewal of the original term.

Tenancy clauses that attract the most questions

The tenancy agreement is the most important document between a landlord and a tenant as it defines the terms upon which a property is let. There used to be lots of complaints about the extensive use of legal jargon and difficulty in understanding what exactly clauses meant. While I would not say that this has been successfully eliminated, the modern tenancy agreement is much clearer than it used to be. The lack of 'hereinafter', 'wherefore', *'ab initio'* (from the start of something), Act of God, and, even more relevant to you and me, 'mesne profits' (use and occupation charge) should be celebrated and the adoption of simple English phrases welcomed.

Questions usually revolve around two key issues with tenancy clauses:

1. Ambiguity

2. Unfairness

These give rise to most legal questions surrounding clauses, although general understanding creeps in a little too.

Let's look at ambiguity first. In contract law this means that the clause is subject to more than one interpretation and is possibly unclear as to what the parties intended. It might also just be the case that the word or phrase is vague or not particularly clear. You must avoid a term like this at all costs if you wish to keep your landlord happy as reliance on such clauses is weighted in favour of the consumer (ie, the tenant). This may mean that the tenant cannot be removed under a break clause because it was badly worded.

For example, the fixed term of an AST is for nine months. The termination clause states: the landlord can terminate the tenancy after the expiry of seven months of the tenancy by giving at least two months' notice. There is no point in this clause as notice is not required to end a fixed term. It has perhaps been care-lessly copied and pasted into a shorter-term tenancy than it was originally included within.

Over the years I have seen some peculiar terms and they just seem to make life more difficult for the landlord. Here are a few examples.

- **The rent of £xxx payable in lunar months.** This one took me by surprise, and it was back in the day when Section 21(4) (a) had to be properly adhered to with the expiry of the notice being the end of a rental period. To serve the notice I had to look up what exactly it meant, and I still didn't know where to start when I discovered it is the time between one new moon and the next. I included a 'savings clause' to avoid problems (adding the wording 'or the day on which a complete period of your tenancy expires next').

- **The landlord may terminate this tenancy with two months' notice to be served at the start of a rental period.** This one seems fine when you read it, but when the start of the rental period is a weekend, service rules play havoc with the service day at weekends, and it is not that simple and can cause a landlord to be annoyed by the delay it causes.

Most tenancy terms are drafted much more simply than they ever used to be, and the term 'with the consent of the landlord, which must not be unreasonably withheld' appears a lot in the body of tenancy agreements to qualify certain terms. This is generally to make them fairer.

Unfairness is the second key area where there can be problems. Contract terms must be clear and expressed in plain language, and fair in the sense that they must not 'prejudice the balance of rights against the consumer' (ie, the tenant). If a term is challenged successfully in court, then the landlord is unable to enforce it. It will depend on the circumstances of the clause and its impact on the tenant as the consumer. This does presume that the landlord is more than just someone with a single property let, that they are more of a businessperson or commercial entity with more perceived 'weight' than the tenant.

If you are requested by a landlord to put in a special term you will now need to be alert to the possibility of it being an unfair term and draft it appropriately. For tenancies prior to 1 October 2015, this unfairness only applied to standard terms and not those specifically negotiated. Examples of clauses very likely to be deemed unfair if challenged would be:

- The landlord or agent can enter the property to undertake an inspection once a month without warning.

- A landlord cannot include a term that allows them to change what was originally let to the tenant. The landlord cannot include a term that allows use of the loft space or to have certain possessions back after the tenancy has begun.

It is a question of balance, and while you can put a clause in that you think may be unfair, unless it is challenged, the landlord can enforce it and the tenant can rely on it if they choose to. If a term is successfully deemed to be unfair it is only that term that will fall away, the rest of the tenancy terms remain in force.

I often get asked about whether a clause can completely exclude the tenant from doing something. This might relate to pets, and the landlord may have a genuine need for this, but it may now be much more likely to be unfair for a blanket prohibition on pets without good reason – not just that the landlord is worried that the property will be 'wrecked' if the tenant is allowed a cat. Pet clauses often raise problems and can be difficult to draft to keep fair. It becomes trickier if you are instructed by your landlord to avoid tenants wanting pets and the tenant asks if a 'therapy' animal is OK.

For example, I recently had a case where the tenant was coming from the United States and asked the landlord to accept her two 'therapy ducks' into his property that she was renting from him. It turned out that the ducks had a seat on the flight over and they were coming over regardless of permission. Documentation from the tenant's medical practitioner was produced to explain the effect of the ducks on the tenant and in the end the landlord allowed it, though somewhat perplexed.

There are all sorts of contractual terms to negotiate, though most are standard and there are numerous precedents for additional clauses that avoid the need in most cases for a brand-new clause to be drafted. If you find yourself not understanding what the clause means or it is not making sense, that is the time to ask for help – don't include the clause and hope nothing happens as there could be problems ahead if challenged.

Notoriously difficult areas of lettings law

There is nothing more satisfying than uncovering then analysing a tricky area of law and then advising someone on it. However, this is generally the job of the lawyer rather than the property professional, and at times you are going to need to pass the matter over to a lawyer for full advice, and with good reason. I will deal with the dangers of you advising on legal issues in Chapter Six.

There are certain areas within lettings law that warrant questions, especially where the circumstances can be extremely variable and require closer examination based on a unique set of facts to every case. There may be cases that arise that ultimately end up with a barrister providing a full opinion on the legal situation. It can be daunting to face something complicated, so knowing which situations you are expected not to know will be a blessing. The following two situations are examples of where you are likely going to need professional legal support for your client.

Regulated tenancies

The first thing to know is that this type of tenancy can no longer be created. They are creatures of the Rent Act 1977 and prior legislation when the purpose behind the legislation was to allow a lifetime security of tenure for renters. They are also referred to as protected tenancies as the security of a tenant is far greater.

The introduction of the Housing Act 1988 on 15 January 1989 changed this and was the radical overhaul of the tenancies available at the time with a shift to short-term tenancies, which you are most familiar with. As time passes, there are fewer regulated tenants around and those that you may have to advise on will become apparent probably because of a succession issue. There will come a time when there will be no regulated tenants, and possibly only assured tenancies that family members enjoy if they meet certain conditions on the death of a regulated tenant.

If you have any experience of regulated tenancies, you will know that there is rarely any paperwork to evidence their terms. The approximate date that the tenant, sometimes surviving tenant, first took up occupation is the biggest clue to knowing that you are dealing with one. The lack of any formal documentation is one reason why difficulties arise in this area, and the other is the very nature of the protection that the tenants are afforded.

I have on a couple of occasions been asked to advise on Protected Shorthold tenancies which were introduced by the Housing Act 1980 until Assured Shorthold Tenancies came in with the Housing Act 1988. Fortunately, the tenancy documentation was to hand and while there are specific rules for notices under these tenancies, I was able to follow those confidently.

Often the questions about regulated tenants are threefold:

1. How do you increase the rent?

2. How do you get possession?

3. Has the original tenancy been succeeded to?

The rent is a 'fair' rent that is assessed, and the legal maximum registered by a Rent Officer from the Valuation Office Agency (VOA). Rent can be increased usually every two years, and the question is often asked because a fair rent is low compared to market rent for regular assured tenancies. There is a form to use to increase rent freely available from www.gov.uk.

How to get possession is more convoluted and is rarely attempted, but it is possible. Section 98 and Schedule 15 to the Rent Act 1977 govern how. Section 98 of the Rent Act 1977 provides that the court must consider it reasonable to make such an order and either (a) the court is satisfied that suitable alternative accommodation is available for the tenant, or will be when the order takes effect, or (b) a discretionary case is made out as in Part I, Schedule 15 of the Rent Act 1977. There are also mandatory cases that can be made out in Part II, Schedule 15 to the Rent Act 1977 in the alternative. Unlike more modern tenancies, high levels of rent arrears do not give a landlord a mandatory right to recover their property.

Rent to Rent

This area ideally needs regulation of its own and can be distressing for landlords. I have been involved in some cases where the landlord's property is innocently let to a company and that company has no intention of occupying the property and promptly lets it out to as many of their own sub-tenants as possible.

Control of the property is lost instantly in these cases, and assured shorthold tenancies will usually be set up for those placed by the company tenant, which gives potential rise to right to rent check problems, overcrowding, HMO regulation breaches, complaints from neighbours because of additional traffic to the property and the list goes on.

I had a particularly bad case where a three-bedroom property had been converted into a seven-bedroom property. The local authority had been contacted by a neighbour querying what was happening at the property as there were numerous people seeming to live there. This resulted in pressure being put on the landlord. As there was obvious overcrowding and no licence held it seemed for the property, it was falling under the definition of a HMO. A regular company let agreement turned into a horror story.

If you find yourself with this scenario not only should you contact a good lawyer, but you should also work with your landlord and the local authority fast to apply for a temporary exemption notice for three months. You then work hard to remove the need for a licence to be required for the property through serving notice and subsequent court action against the tenant. The notice can be extended for a further three months subject to the local authority considering that there are exceptional circumstances to do so.

It is a particularly stressful time for the landlord as nothing court related is ever quick enough for them, and all the while the neighbours may continue to complain, and the original company tenant may also continue to secure numerous rents at the landlord's expense as the tenant usually stops paying rent too.

Rent to Rent is now regarded as a specific type of arrangement and should be set up with a commercial agreement as it is a business run by a company which then controls the property. That agreement should allow for the leasing of the property. There are agencies whose business models work in a way which guarantees their landlords the rental payments, and they act as the tenant effectively and place tenants in the property. It can work well at a professional level, but the consensus is that it is open to a lot of unscrupulous misuse and needs proper regulating.

Your job as a property professional and my job as a legal advisor are generally quite different. Our continual professional development to enhance our knowledge and understanding of the law is mutual. You need to recognise the legal issues where it is appropriate to direct your client to an expert in the field to resolve properly. I go to a specialist barrister when I need an in-depth look at an area of law, and it supports my client in establishing what risks there are associated with any litigation. For you, advising a landlord that they should be taking legal advice is no bad thing and should be regarded as the best advice you can give on occasion. It can save you time, will properly support your landlord, possibly save the landlord thousands of pounds to know the legal position, keep you professional and less stressed, and maintain your business relationship with that landlord. Remember that sometimes implementation and additional advice is best left to another expert.

Surprising facts in lettings law

Uncovering the law can lead to some surprising findings. Sometimes you do not go looking for the answers to certain legal questions, and they can remain puzzling. I thought I would end this chapter by mentioning three such legal areas, which once you know of will further improve your understanding of why certain aspects of your job exist as they do.

Abandonment

This term is frequently used in the industry and happens when a tenant does not appear to be living in a property but there is a tenancy in place. I deal with abandonment in more detail in the last section of this book about practical resolutions to situations, but the key thing here is to understand that in law there is no legal definition.

You may be unsure what to do, but your landlord wants to stop the rent arrears growing if the tenant has gone and is urging you to do something about it. Can you, if the tenant is no longer in the property, change the locks? You are torn between knowing you shouldn't and knowing what to do for the best.

I will just remind you of the law at this point to legally terminate the occupation of a residential assured tenant:

Section 5 of the Housing Act 1988:

1. An assured tenancy cannot be brought to an end by the landlord except by -

    a. obtaining—

        i. an order of the court for possession of the dwelling-house under Section 7 or 21, and

        ii. the execution of the order[13]

There is also surrender by a tenant, but you need this to be offered and accepted unequivocally. Without knowing the tenant's intentions this may not be possible. You are treading on unlawful eviction territory, and this is where 'abandonment' comes in to try and bridge the gap and flush out what the situation is. However, you need to get it right. Tenants can 'reappear' after some weeks claiming they were abroad or unwell, and if you have nothing to indicate they had previously abandoned the property, you are running a risk.

---

13 Housing Act 1988, Section 5, www.legislation.gov.uk/ukpga/1988/50/section/5, accessed 7 July 2022

Insurance

This is often a surprising one as we do not stop to think about it. The question is usually: Does the landlord have to have house insurance?

Most tenancies will mention insurance at some point, often to warn the tenant that if they do anything which renders the policy void or triggers a claim resulting in increased premiums (if this can be proved) the tenant will be held liable. This relates to building insurance, and you will be comfortable advising tenants that it would be sensible to have their own contents insurance for their occupation.

The question is whether you can insist on insurance for landlord or tenant, and the answer is no. This must be checked with landlords as where there is a mortgage over the property, the mortgagee generally insists on buildings insurance being in place to protect their security.

The only mandatory insurance in this country is motor insurance, which you must hold to drive a motor vehicle lawfully. Every other insurance is a personal lifestyle choice. Tenancy agreements must allow forms of insurance to be 'recommended', rather than insisted upon.

Long leases

There is a little-known fact that applies to 'long' leases that you should at least be aware of, as one day you may be asked for a much longer lease than you are generally familiar with. I have advised on a couple over the years and generally they are put in place for large properties with numerous bedrooms, a swimming pool, stables, a converted barn or a lot of land. This will likely be a property of some grandeur that the owners want to let on a much longer period to prevent regular tenant change as it can take time to find new tenants, and there are usually many specific terms to be adhered to by tenants.

What is a long residential lease? Generally, this is a term of more than twenty-one years with a low rent, but I am not referring to these. Tenancies that are being negotiated at over seven years, perhaps eight to ten years, are those where there is a change to the usual way in which a repairing covenant will work.

With regular, shorter tenancy agreements be they AST or common law, you know that Section 11 of the Landlord and Tenant Act 1985 applies to provide an implied covenant for a landlord:

- To keep in repair the structure and exterior of the dwelling-house (including drains, gutters and external pipes)

- To keep in repair and proper working order the installations in the dwelling-house for the supply of water, gas and electricity and for sanitation (including basins, sinks, baths and sanitary conveniences, but not other fixtures, fittings and appliances for making use of the supply of water, gas or electricity)

- To keep in repair and proper working order the installations in the dwelling-house for space heating and heating water[14]

The key takeaway here is that Section 11 only applies to tenancies and leases that are less than seven years. The general rule is set out in Section 13 of the Landlord and Tenant Act 1985, where it states: 'Section 11 (repairing obligations) applies to a lease of a dwelling-house granted on or after the 24 October 1961 for a term of less than seven years.'[15]

The shift of the responsibility for disrepair in leases of seven years or more is to the tenant, and this is important when negotiating such a tenancy. Whatever you may negotiate in this situation make sure it is spelt out in the tenancy documents and everybody understands what their responsibilities are.

Summary

I have provided you with a sounder basis for questions that are largely due to a gap in knowledge of contractual law. You must accept the areas of law that you should direct your landlord to a legal adviser for and allow them to uncover the legal position fully. Given that even I seek formal legal advice on occasion, you should never feel that this an indication of

---

14 Landlord and Tenant Act 1985, Section 11, www.legislation.gov.uk/ukpga/1985/70/section/11, accessed 7 July 2022
15 Landlord and Tenant Act 1985, Section 13, www.legislation.gov.uk/ukpga/1985/70/section/13, accessed 7 July 2022

failure because you do not know the answer. By doing so, you will keep your stress levels lower and do the right thing for your landlord in ensuring that they get the best professional advice from someone who knows and can deliver it succinctly, correctly and fast.

I have only touched the surface as contract law is a broad and often complicated subject that can prove tricky at times. You now know:

- What your questions reveal

- Why your knowledge of contract law is a major factor in the questions you ask

- The principles of forming a contract

- Tenancy clauses that cause the most problems and why, be that ambiguity or unfairness

- Areas of lettings law when it is entirely right to seek legal advice

- Three areas of lettings law that can be surprising and improve your understanding further

SIX
Share The Solution

The purpose behind the next step in the HOUSE rules, is a reminder to share what you find out, otherwise you are not recognising the value in the answers to your questions to you and your business, or allowing others to flourish along with you.

There will be those inner voices at work resisting the need to share solutions while you build your own reputation or empire and show everyone what you are made of, and that you are the fountain of knowledge. It does not need to be like this, and you only have yourself to blame if you choose to work in this way. You may find yourself alienated, lacking time to spend on your business as you try and do everything, stressed as a result, and most importantly restricting your ability to grow by not sharing those pearls of wisdom you are capturing within your day.

There are others of you who will openly share what they have learned and love bringing others along with them. It feels good, improves knowledge in the workplace and is much more enriching. Sharing legal answers and solutions can have huge benefits at whatever level of your professional life you are at, and I want to look at why with you.

Time well spent

The phrase 'knowledge is power' is generally accredited to Sir Francis Bacon in his 1597 book, *Meditationes Sacrae and Human Philosophy*.[16] Or as Thomas Jefferson said in the early 1800s, 'Sharing knowledge is the key to unlocking that power.'[17]

I want you to remember these words when you receive a legal answer which has allowed you to progress with your work. Do not simply hold on to it and get on – share it. It does not have to be instantly, but make sure you spread the knowledge and support others in your business or working day. This could be when you have a coffee break and are in the kitchen, or a quick mention of it as you find something out during the day that you know will ease the stress of others who don't know how to do what you now do.

---

16 F Bacon, *Meditationes Sacrae and Human Philosophy* (1597), https://en.wikipedia.org/wiki/Scientia_potentia_est, accessed 7 July 2022

17 T Jefferson, American president and Enlightenment writer, www.monticello.org/site/research-and-collections/knowledge-power-quotation, accessed 7 July 2022

It sounds obvious, but some days you are so locked into what you are doing that you don't think of anyone else. It is a wasted opportunity not to share new knowledge, however small, as you never know what piece of information might be useful to another person. You may even formalise discussion by allowing time in a regular office meeting, or similar, to update on legal matters.

It is a known fact that knowledge which you gather from multiple people who tell you the same thing is far more reliable as shared knowledge and is essential to your learning and growth. Sharing is also often reciprocated as you gain the trust of your colleagues.

If I find something out that I feel is important for my team to know I will share it immediately during the working day, which is the beauty of an email as it becomes a point of reference. If it is an area of law which takes a little longer to understand and apply, I usually add it to our team meeting agenda, and it is covered as a mini legal update to ensure everyone knows what to do if they need to apply it. If I get asked a great question at a legal update I give, I bring it back to the team as it enhances the depth of understanding of the topic. I positively encourage the whole team to talk among themselves whenever they come across what for them is a problem – it's faster, more satisfying learning from within and from the experience of others, and you are more likely to apply it and remember it in a practical context.

I am forever learning, and you should feel the same and be willing to share freely the legal gems that you pick up as you go along to becoming an even better property professional. It's how friendships are built, how you get better at what you do and how promotions are gained.

If, for example, you discover exactly why you should use as many grounds as possible relating to rent arrears when serving a Section 8 – Grounds 8, 10 and 11 or a combination of 8 with 10 or 11 – make sure you tell everyone you work with about it. Some of them may know they have to use them all, but some may not know why, and it is this critical element that makes your understanding strong if you need to serve one in the future. It would hurt if you knew this and then you find one of your colleagues did not and it caused a possession claim to fail when the landlord decided to act on it of their own accord. In fact, it will not stay contained for long as the landlord will point the finger squarely at you for not advising them fully on this and including the discretionary Grounds 10 and/or 11 to prevent the whole claim being dismissed if the rent arrears are brought down below the two-month mark at the time of the court hearing.

By sharing legal knowledge, you save time for your colleagues by telling them something you have found out as soon as possible. Their confidence will grow, you will remain professional and knowledgeable in front of your clients, you will help to avoid mistakes and you will feel great. What could be more satisfying?

Be careful how you use your answer

I have positively encouraged you to share your legal knowledge from answers you receive, but like everything there are always some exceptions to the rule.

One of the key areas I must highlight is the temptation to provide legal advice to your clients. I often tell my team that while I hope it never happens, they should never gloss over or hide something that they may have done wrong. It takes a brave person to admit to a mistake, but far better that it is mentioned immediately when it happens than further down the line when more damage has been done.

You and I are only humans, and mistakes are going to happen on occasion. In my case, professional indemnity insurance is there to protect and help me and others in the legal profession. For agencies there are redress schemes providing access to a property ombudsman, and public indemnity insurance for those moments within your business when things don't quite go to plan.

To think you are perfect is dangerous, but you should work diligently and to the best of your ability. Should anything untoward arise, you need to address it fast and, most importantly, learn from your mistakes.

I know from experience that doing something wrong is awful. You do take it personally despite what everyone tells you, and you can beat yourself up for hours and days over how stupid you were or how on earth you missed something or typed something wrong. It is the hardest thing to accept an error, but if you analyse why it happened and put procedures in place for not doing it again, you have learned from it. Success comes from the failures provided you do act upon it in a way to reduce the risk of it happening again.

This may sound dramatic, but the serious message is that the insurance for you and me is different. I am legally qualified and, even if I was not, I am working for a company that has the right cover for me providing legal advice. It is what I do. In the lettings industry, if you decide to provide legal advice, however innocently and with the best of intention that you may give it, there could be repercussions far more widely felt by the business if you discover that your insurance does not cover legal advice.

I can recall several occasions when I have been contacted about completion of a court claim form. This starts the alarm bells ringing, not just if I am speaking to a landlord who may not be my client at that point, but also when you as property professionals start asking questions about what goes where. I will always explore what you are trying to do and why, and, if necessary, explain why it is not such a good idea to help with this and that the landlord should take proper legal advice or do it themselves. This is mainly intended to protect you as the foreseeable losses which may arise from filling a court form in incorrectly based on your advice could be substantial. Using the Section 8 example from earlier in this chapter, the increasing rent arrears, the further delay when the claim is struck out or dismissed to get things back on track, and the landlord's costs in issuing the claim will be sizable and it will be left to you to cover those losses. This is coupled with irritation that completing a claim form is firmly part of a legal advisor's work and asking for help to complete any court form is not a proper legal question. Politely saying that you are unable to assist on this occasion is the right answer every time in these situations.

Possibly worse than helping in this manner, in terms of professional embarrassment both in front of the court and potentially your client, is agreeing to attend a court hearing to support the landlord's claim. If you agree to support your landlord and attend court for them, make sure that the landlord goes with you, and you do not end up representing them on your own.

In the County Court, if your landlord is a company client, the ability to be heard by the court is through a legal representative only, unless you get special dispensation. Consequently, if your landlord is expecting you to attend, you may end up with the judge refusing to hear you on your own as you are not a legal representative. It can cause an adjournment at best and a claim being dismissed at worst.

On the other hand, even if you attend with the landlord who is a director of the company the same thing can happen. If you manage to get past the initial problem of a lack of legal representative, if you have helped complete your client's court claim form incorrectly and it transpires that at the hearing that error becomes the basis of the claim being dismissed, you are going to be blamed immediately – a public humiliation.

No matter how kind and helpful you are wanting to be, sometimes declining to help is the best way forward, even if you do know the answer or think you know how to do something and want to share it. What you don't know you don't know, and stepping into a lawyer's shoes for a few minutes can prove painful. You need to be confident saying no and in recognising when it is entirely appropriate to refer your client to a lawyer.

The limitations of principal and agent

If you are a property professional who works as a letting agent, then you are governed by an area of law known as 'agency law'. This is based on a principal-agent relationship that allows one person legal authority to act for another and bind a third party. In the world of letting agents the landlord is the principal, you are the agent and you are appointed officially as the agent through your terms of business (TOB). There is a Latin maxim upon which the law of agency is based, and in English it is translated as 'he who acts through another is deemed in law to do it himself'.

As lettings law develops, more and more legislation includes agents as well as landlords being able to do various things. However, it can also leave you liable if something is not carried out correctly or if it is outside the scope of your authority set out in your TOB.

It is clear from some of the questions I have taken over the years that you may forget this relatively unspoken about area of law that governs your business with the landlords you act for. Where there has been a challenge to what you have carried out, or the way in which you did or did not do something for your landlord and 'negligence' is being alleged, you must consider what your duty was and the extent of that duty. You starting point is your TOB.

You need to be aware of the limitations associated with your agency appointment, so that when you do get legal answers to certain aspects of your work, you remember to ensure that before you get too enthusiastic about sharing an answer and getting on with things, you are authorised to do it.

For most of your work relating to simple ASTs for terms of three years or less, your TOB, which is a contractual document, will be sufficient to authorise you to sign off such tenancy agreements on your landlord's behalf. This is an area that attracts questions sometimes and it should be stated within your agreement with the landlord if authority to sign agreements has been given. If a landlord wants you to sign off tenancies that are over three years which must be by deed, you must complete a deed to be given permission to do this. This is provided under the Power of Attorney Act 1971 and requires additional paperwork such as a power of attorney.

If instructed to do something, you will have to ask yourself whether you have the authority to do so. Authority is a key aspect of agency law and there are three different types:

1. Express authority is whatever is written in your service agreement.

2. Implied authority is where you act reasonably in a way that is incidental to the execution of your express authority.

3. Restricted authority is authority to act only to a certain point.

This is what makes the content of your TOB so important. If it is not clear and comprehensive, there may be problems ahead in knowing whether or not you were authorised to undertake certain work. Implied authority can help, particularly if you can demonstrate how you have always worked with a given landlord in a certain way in the past. Restricted authority may be shown through the limited terms relating, for example, to a 'tenant find only' agreement which does not then involve you getting involved in the management of the property, including disrepair. Using a wide term like 'to manage the property on a day-to-day basis' will allow you as agent to do everything that you need to ensure the property is managed daily. It is not likely to extend to the issue of legal proceedings for possession. You would have to ensure that this was put expressly into your TOB, but this would be unlikely for insurance reasons.

I have been asked specific questions about whether you as an agent can do something, such as organising a contractor. However, I cannot answer many questions without sight of your TOB. You need to look carefully at whether you have any of the types of authority to do what you are asking. One classic example of this is where you cannot get in touch with your landlord, and you need to get some disrepair work done at the property. If your TOB only provides you with authority up to a certain value of work and you need to exceed it, should you choose to get the work done you are running the risk that the landlord will not ratify your action and possibly hold you liable for the cost of the work over that authorised. You might be able, if available, to rely on another term that if in emergency such a cost limit can be exceeded, but usually you would not have the funds on account so you must be careful.

Further areas that you need to be very clear about within your TOB where you are only finding a tenant for a landlord are:

- Who is responsible for right to rent checks if you are in England and only finding a tenant for your landlord

- Whether you will 'receive' the deposit from a tenant

Both can end up problematic for an agent and create potential liability unless you state who will do what.

Most of your authorised actions will be covered within your service agreement, TOB or management agreement. However you refer to it, this is the contract which binds you and your landlord as principal and agent. Before you share a great legal answer, check your service agreement to ensure that you are authorised to do what you are about to do.

Be proactive and create new procedures

The last piece of the share element of the HOUSE rules is to get creative with your legal answers. This is sharing with impact. Consider whether you can:

- Usefully take action to ensure that your work colleagues know how something is to be done

- Change a procedure or in-house policy to reflect what you now know

- Create a checklist for a part of your process that will make sure nothing is left out

- Add a regular legal issue or legal update item to your team meeting agenda and see if others are having the same problem and jointly work something out to reduce risk

- Regularly review your TOB

- Ensure you are aware of how agency law works and refer to the TOB when necessary to check if you are authorised

These points may sound obvious, but busy days can mean that your answers are not necessarily shared or acted upon to benefit others. You move on to the next thing with every good intention, but this never changes anything.

Some areas of law are complicated, or at least have numerous steps which you must follow to the letter to get something carried out correctly. You may have to get the legislation out and highlight everything that you need to do and either build this into your general work process or create a flowchart for you and your colleagues to follow. There is no point reinventing the wheel, so see if there are any such flowcharts already in circulation. Flowcharts are mainly for where there are lots of possibilities or it is a complex or cumbersome area of law, such as licensing arrangements for HMOs or serving valid Section 21 notices. You will undoubtedly have your own for tenancy set-up, move-in and check-out, and rent arrears procedures, among others. These can be extended to be utilised for legal issues that you find are important to tackle in a certain way so that you are not forgetting something important that could impact later. This might be a quick reference sheet for the grounds for Section 8 notices, for example, or prompts as you complete an AST to remind everyone to check if the parties want email included as a method of service or not.

If you can show a procedure is in place to reduce the risk of something going wrong, this can help with obtaining competitive insurance or an industry standard. Anything that reduces the risk of there being a claim against you is worth considering, so rather than wait until something is missed or goes wrong, take a simple step to avoid the need for it to happen in the first place. This is the proactivity I am referring to, purposefully sharing the answers to your legal questions and using them in helpful and meaningful ways to support you and your business.

Summary

Sharing the solution to your legal problems provides you with the perfect excuse to ask the questions in the first place. Share the answers you receive and enhance the operation of you and your business for the better. You should remember that:

- Your time becomes meaningful when you do not hold on to the answer purely for your own need

- You should be smart with your legal answers given that time is such a precious commodity

- To share is to reduce risk for you and your colleagues in the workplace

- Your insurance is unlikely to cover you for giving legal advice from your legal answers

- You operate within the law of agency, so be confident knowing when to instruct an expert to ensure the job is done properly

- Through changes to procedure, documented process, supportive prompts when completing forms or documents, or simply talking about legal issues regularly at team meetings or catch-ups, you will sharpen the way your business runs

SEVEN
Evaluate

Now that you have usefully shared your legal answer and started realising the potential in doing so, the last piece of the HOUSE rules is to Evaluate legal issues and the answers to any that you need to ask about.

You may be wondering what it means to evaluate. What I mean is that you should form an idea of the value of an answer:

- Is it wider reaching than a one-off answer?

- What are the implications of the answer for the business?

- Can the answer save your landlords' costs?

- Can the answer reduce risk with a task you carry out regularly?

- How can you best put the answer into the business to support you?

This is not an exhaustive list but provides some pointers as to how you can evaluate what new knowledge you obtain and be able to act upon some of the answers. This chapter looks at how you can work with relevant legal answers and create good practice in the workplace. I also direct you to some resources to support you in this and shape the way you do things.

Working with your answers

You are not going to be able to use every legal answer you receive for the greater good of your workplace. This is not realistic. The evaluation part of the HOUSE rules is to ensure that whenever you do need to seek legal advice, you at least consider the worth of that information.

In a business context, evaluating is working out whether practices that are in place are good, bad or indifferent, and striving to improve those. Aside from financial targets, which in themselves may be driven by the underlying practices the business has in place, the focus can be on various aspects of the work you do with the purpose of improving the effectiveness of tasks you carry out or even the speed with which those tasks are completed.

If, for example, you wanted to work on gathering the prescribed legal documents during the set-up stage of the tenancy – the EPC, the gas safety certificate and the *How To Rent Guide* – you would first analyse what is generally done in the office, seek feedback from colleagues who carry out these tasks to see where the process might be made easier or quicker, develop a plan of change and finally measure how successful changes are by comparing the former system with the new process over a given time period. You will likely end up with your top three rated contractors for the EPC and gas safety certificates being in an accessible format which can be easily consulted, a rule that you use the live *How To Rent Guide* link on the www.gov.uk website to ensure you have the latest edition and a checklist to tick these documents off on the file so anyone looking at it can see what has been done.

With legal issues, you should be able to notice, and measure, when questions are arising frequently in relation to the same legal topic. Your focus is then on gaining greater explanation or deeper understanding of that issue, which may involve some formal training. You may decide that a checklist or formal prompting with short explanations are required within a process. This is to make tasks easier and reduce the risk of something going wrong.

One legal requirement that generates regular legal questions is right to rent checks for those based in England. With Brexit and the pandemic, the checks have undergone some considerable changes and, if anything, have fast-forwarded the need for the Home Office to implement a digital checking process.

Right to rent is a procedure that is essential for letting properties in England to adults eighteen years of age and over. The key aim is to create a statutory excuse to avoid a breach of the rules. This is an area of law that is supported by several resources – a Landlord's Guide, a User Guide and a Code of Conduct are available from www.gov.uk. These need to be a part of the evaluation process in your own workplace, as the User Guide sets out the documents in Lists A and B and what combination of these you need if you cannot use digital evidence of a prospective tenant's right to rent. It is an area where a helpline is in operation at the Home Office and further, when you need to use the landlord checking service, you should get a response within forty-eight hours. You should take advantage of the information and support available and ensure everyone uses it who may need to.

HMOs is another area that is a good one for evaluation if you deal with HMOs regularly. With selective and additional licensing schemes springing up all over the country you need to be particularly savvy when it comes to checking whether the property you are letting requires a licence. Given the constant changes it is easy to miss the requirements in some authorities unless you have a solid procedure which is used for every instruction that could possibly be an HMO. The legal questions that are generally asked on HMOs relate to a tenant who does not seem to reside in the property but has moved a lot of people in to sub-let.

The property was never an HMO but ends up being one due to the tenant's breach. Using the information I provided in Chapter Five about rent to rent, you should ensure that you can recognise this legal issue fast and put in place a tight procedure that you follow as you may not have much warning and the situation cannot be allowed to continue due to the serious consequences associated with running an HMO without a licence, albeit that you and the landlord are involuntarily placed in this position. It may be that upon evaluation you decide that this scenario if it arises will require legal advice, or you have specific steps to implement that include reporting to a senior member of the business if appropriate and telephone numbers to ring to contact key parties, such as the local authority, as soon as you realise what has happened.

The two legal topics addressed here will result in important processes being introduced within your workplace. They are good examples of legal issues where you should utilise the answers obtained from experts and knowledge from every online resource to devise a simple way to deal consistently with queries that will arise, be that in-house or from a legal advisor.

Implement best practice and maintain it

To extend the evaluation process and solidify it using your legal answers in how you work, you must familiarise yourself with and ensure you are matching best practice within the lettings industry. There are several professional bodies created to promote best practice in the private rented sector and these are:

- Royal Institution of Chartered Surveyors (RICS)

- Association of Residential Letting Agents (ARLA) (Propertymark)

- National Association of Estate Agents (NAEA) (Propertymark)

- Safeagent – previously National Approved Letting Scheme (NALS)

- The Law Society

Raising standards is high on the agenda of these bodies as is the introduction of the Private Rented Sector Code of Best Practice which those bodies, along with numerous other leading industry bodies and the Minister for Housing, consulted on and originally published in 2014. The Property Ombudsman also has the Code of Practice for Residential Lettings Agents and ARLA a Code of Practice. Eventually each redress scheme will share the same code.

These approved codes of practice support regulations, but it is not a statutory requirement to follow them. If court process was taken though, the code can be used as evidence of a contravention of a statutory requirement. Not following the code does not automatically mean you are liable in any court proceedings, but it does not look good.

The codes tend to be revised to reflect legislative changes so are a great starting point for evaluation to check that you are measuring up to expectations within your lettings setting. They are extensive and cover everything that you are expected to do as a property professional.

What you are looking to achieve from implementing best practice is a way of doing things that gives you better results. You might gain a legal answer from which you could improve such practice, but you could easily find other best practice examples from business literature and magazines and websites. Learning about other businesses who might be pioneering a new software platform or way of doing something might provide an idea that you too want to apply in your business. You can be curious about the best and adopt those best practices which resonate and help you the most.

There is plenty of guidance readily available in the lettings sector as to what best practice should look like. With an increasing number of 'prop tech' businesses appearing in the market, there are some great ideas to be considered for all sorts of processes that makes it easier to keep up with the changing legislation. From end-to-end workflow management for repairs to properties to accounting solutions there is a plethora of choice to support you. Many, if not all, of these companies promise automatic updated legislation, keeping you compliant with required regulations and keeping you worry free in that regard. It's all about working smart and exploring the offerings available.

A positive first step to implement best practice with ease and allow your business to succeed.

Best practice can evolve in your workplace through case law. One such area is the change-over of multiple sharers and the case study which is set out in Chapter One. As a result of the influential rather than precedent *Sturgiss* case, the way in which you handle sharer changes has been discussed in some detail. A deed of assignment may become the new norm for tenant churn, rather than a new tenancy and all that entails with deposit, security of tenure, and inventory. The case highlighted omissions by the landlord in dealing with such changes and allowed the legal issue to be judicially discussed. This in turn allows you as property professionals to evaluate the way you do this element of your work and make it as neat, cost efficient, and legally effective as possible for you. All that is then required is regular review to ensure you are keeping up to date with any changes.

The benefits of e-signing

There is a growing trend for electronic signatures to be used for the important part of tenancy completion. The Electronic Communications Act 2000 at Section 7 (42) provides for 'the admissibility of electronic signatures and related certificates in legal proceedings'. E-signing has been acceptable in legal circles for years.

E-signing has been embraced by property professionals as the predominant method for entering into a tenancy agreement. The legal requirements surrounding service of various documents on the tenant have been neatly incorporated into this process as it provides a simple way to show that the tenant has received all key documents. Every page included in the electronic envelope with the tenancy agreement is linked by the same marking and there is a completion certificate page showing the signatory's email address, IP address, and date and time of accessing the document and signing. This has been an industry exercise in evaluating and simplifying the area of completion of the tenancy.

Legal issues relating to the order of signing for guarantors if you use e-signing is resolved by setting the signing order. This, as I have previously explained, is imperative if you are using contracts for guarantees.

Deeds of guarantee have traditionally needed to have 'wet-ink' signatures due to the need for a witness to that signature. This has always served to slow down the process of executing the deed due to the reliance on the physical presence of the signatory and witness. There is no precedent for witnessing electronically yet, but there are definite moves in known e-sign circles ready to introduce a way in which deeds can be signed and witnessed electronically by capturing that the signatory and witness are in the same location and can complete at the same time. Even this tricky area may soon have an acceptable answer.

The e-signing of tenancy agreements allows all the legal documents to be included with the tenancy and ensures that you remain compliant at this critical stage by not forgetting any. There is further easy scope to include other documentation. Many of you already include the EICR which became compulsory for all tenancies from 1 April 2021 and needs to be served on the tenant. If the EICR becomes another document that must be evidenced as being served before a valid Section 21 notice can be served, then that compliance box is already ticked by using e-signing.

In court process, the accelerated claim form requires dates for the service of all key documents that demonstrate that service of the Section 21 notice, upon which that possession procedure is solely based, is valid. Given that the court paperwork must be scrutinised by a district judge, the use of the certificate of completion and the documents that display the same envelope reference throughout is a definite win to make it easier for the judiciary to accept that the tenant has received all legally required documents. The use of this technology can help your landlords when they are faced with a court claim.

When you are evaluating your processes and looking at the legal issues that cause those problems or are riskier to get right, it can be effective while developing your possible solutions to consider and then select technology to resolve them. The technology must meet your needs, and to some extent future needs, and should be within your budget. Get it right and it can be game-changing.

Using primary authority partnerships

A valuable resource in your armoury when dealing with legal issues and establishing answers is the Primary Authority Scheme (PAS). Introduced in 2009, it is designed to help you as property professionals to remain compliant with the regulation that you work within.

PAS is a government-backed scheme administered by the Department for Business, Energy and Industrial Strategy and specifically by the Office for Product Safety and Standards (OPSS). You can be any type of business to enter a partnership with regulators operating as primary authorities, which includes county, district and unitary councils and fire and rescue authorities. You can belong to a trade association that has an existing co-ordinated partnership such as ARLA Propertymark and Safeagent (NALS). There is a public register that you can use to see whether a company or organisation has a partnership in place. For those agencies with multiple branches, it can provide a consistent approach to issues wherever the agency is trading in England and Wales and the whole business can keep compliant using the primary authority.

Why am I promoting this relatively understated resource within the evaluation part of the HOUSE rules? In lettings you know that there are numerous pieces of legislation to ensure compliance with and PAS covers environmental health, trading standards and fire safety. You can just be registered for those that are relevant to lettings. Propertymark, for example, partners with Warwickshire County Council Trading Standards, as it is this area that tends to invite more interpretation on regulations for the industry than any other. All businesses with Propertymark protection are automatically enrolled into the partnership and their website details those areas upon which the PAS has given advice. Anything from consumer protection advice to general property transactions to Universal Credit issues.

The Primary Authority's advice creates a consistent approach to certain aspects of regulation and enforcement. Their advice could include interpretation of legislation, the legal obligation that your business must adhere to or assessment of the procedures you have in place to ensure you are legally compliant.

One Primary Authority may not interpret something the same way as another, and the advice given can lead to legal action where the advice is not followed. You can rest assured that other local authorities must contact the Primary Authority before any legal action can be taken, and, provided you have followed the guidance, it is unlikely any further action will be taken.

Here is a working example:

QUESTION: Should agents tell a prospective tenant that the property they are seeking to let has been burgled multiple times?

ANSWER: Yes. The situation was considered by The Property Ombudsman in December

2013 and more recently advice from a Primary Authority given to support it. You should, where acting as an agent, 'provide all material information that the average consumer needs to take an informed transactional decision' under the Consumer Protection from Unfair Trading Regulations 2008. It was regarded as a 'misleading omission' not to have told the tenants before they entered into the tenancy agreement.

You should give this information to a tenant, particularly if as in this case the security measures that the police had suggested had not been implemented by the landlord.

Where a Primary Authority partnership is in place you should check historic advice and use it to evaluate your own response to how you deal with that aspect of the law. It is a tool which you should feel confident using for the uniform approach which it provides. It is a great resource that many businesses may not be taking advantage of which could expose them to prosecution for noncompliance.

Summary

The final evaluation part of the HOUSE rules can elevate your business if used correctly. The Evaluation step goes much further than simple sharing of your legal answers. It provides the focus that you need to support you and all those working in your business to shape and drive your business forward. Remember to:

- Identify those areas of law which regularly demand a process and implement one

- Use the available resources within the lettings industry to streamline your business quickly and efficiently

- Become confidently compliant in the areas of lettings law that can prove tricky and risky by using resources and technology wherever possible

- Consider using Primary Authority Partnerships for consistent best practice solutions

PART THREE
APPLICATION OF YOUR ANSWERS

At this stage you are aware of the legal questions that cause you the most problems and have a working knowledge of the HOUSE rules and their application. This will help you ask great questions and use your answers to best effect.

In this final section of the book, I take an important look at the way you apply the answers. I like to regard my legal answers as being as clear and as practical as they can be for your own understanding and use. How well the answer is implemented is down to you.

I explore how you can make more informed decisions when faced with a potentially difficult tenant, a situation where there appears to be no viable way out apart from taking a risk, or a landlord who may be pushing for an outcome that you are not happy to enact and so you need to protect your actions. I also provide you with a light-hearted look at how maddening some tenancies can prove and yet the law can still be readily applied. I'll also look at how you can easily ensure that you are compliant as a business, and why this is important. I conclude with how you can use legal answers to shape and support you and your business whether you are an owner or not.

EIGHT

Textbook Answer Or Practical Solution

For many, studying law can be arduous, and to some extent tedious, as the subject areas are vast and the relevant cases and legislation voluminous. By far the hardest part is bringing your book knowledge to life when you finish your studies and get your first job in the real world. Application is everything. From textbook to everyday situations, how you interpret and apply the correct law to your case is the real skill.

My purpose here is to make you as a property professional confident in assessing legal situations that you meet in your daily work. There will be a textbook answer, but when your landlord is facing a situation that could easily be resolved by defying that answer and applying some common sense, which way do you turn?

There are several dilemmas common to lettings law where you are faced with textbook application or a sensible solution, and I explore these along with the way to approach such situations to get the best result for your landlord. There are also cases where things become difficult for you when the landlord is looking to point the finger in your direction for some, or all, of the blame, and the word negligence looms. Or perhaps you need to resolve a situation fast because the 'A1' reference obtained for a tenant has not prepared you for the barrage of complaints that come your way from that individual unexpectedly, and you are looking to do your best for the landlord.

By textbook application, I do not just mean literally what the legal books say but also the general expected route that you would follow if you were to implement the usual process fully as required. This could mean a claims process in a professional indemnity situation for example, and application perhaps of an alternative method to avoid that.

Assess the risk

Whenever you are about to go 'off-piste' and sort a situation out that you either think is not strictly legal, or may not be, you must always apply the same thinking to such steps and assess the risk.

Assessing the risk is critical. You must consider what could happen to the landlord, and you to some extent, if the worst thing happened and the action taken was found to be unlawful. There could be major implications for both you and the landlord. This will become easier to grasp as I explore actual events which will be familiar. What you want to ensure you end up with is the position in which you present the various potential outcomes to the landlord, and you then step back and allow the decision to rest solely with the landlord. If you have clearly set out all the options, including the textbook one, then you will have a much easier time should the most serious upshot materialise. Without offering all options, you may find that you are easily blamed for not explaining the worst-case scenario or for not letting the landlord know of the penalty they might face if the tenant responds in a certain way. This usually results in a complaint, or even a claim in negligence, which you want to avoid and can avoid with some preparation.

The Legionella Risk Assessment is a legal obligation for landlords under the Health and Safety at Work Act 1974 and must be carried out at the start of a new tenancy on behalf of your landlord. Its purpose is to minimise the chance of anyone using the property contracting what is the potentially fatal Legionnaires' disease.

You need to carry out your own risk assessment on the facts that have arisen in your scenario with the purpose of minimising the chances of there being any repercussions to the landlord for not having followed the letter of the law. In each case you must:

- Explore all the facts

- Weigh up the likelihood and severity of risks

- Put in place precautions that may be required

- Carry out checks to fully appreciate the risk

- Report fully and concisely to the landlord to enable them to decide how to proceed

- Treat every case on its own set of facts

These steps are self-explanatory. The latter point is of particular importance, as there may be subtle differences between the last case and the current one which could raise or lower the assessed risk accordingly. Do not simply do the same thing as you did before without fully investigating whether that is the best option.

What you are aiming for is to take the action that is proportionate to the level of risk. If the level of risk cannot be lowered sufficiently then your advice must revert to the textbook answer. Better to be safe than sorry.

For example, a situation where you cannot take any risk is when you know that the tenant has been sent to prison. You may discover this fact from a story printed in local or national media, or from a relative or friend of the tenant. The tenant's principal home remains the property that they rented, even if you know that the sentence is going to keep the tenant at His Majesty's pleasure for some time. The tenancy does not end based on this eventuality, and you must apply Section 5 of the Housing Act 1988 and ensure that the landlord obtains a court order and enforces it to recover possession of the property legally. You will need to serve a statutory notice, be that Section 8 or Section 21 depending on the facts at the property which is the tenant's last known place of residence. It would be best also to contact the tenant if you can. You may have to rely on a relative or the central service for HM Prisons to discover which prison the tenant is in. If the tenant has a long sentence, communication will be key to establishing whether the tenant is prepared to surrender the tenancy legally. This could be helpful with removal of possessions. If you take court proceedings and enforce the order, you will end up with their possessions still in situ and may have to sort storage for the landlord. Surrender, however, requires an offer to do so from the tenant and acceptance by the landlord, so communication is key. Surrender is also the best way to avoid the time and cost associated with taking the court process. You cannot in this scenario simply take back possession.

Another common example of needing to consider the 'textbook' answer verses practical solution is when tenants leave personal possessions in the property. There are many variables here, especially as the law that covers this area is not clear.

I doubt anyone has not experienced, at least to some degree, a tenant leaving personal items at the property either at the end of the tenancy term, after formal eviction or during a tenancy when you have reason to believe the tenant may have abandoned the property. The problem is, whenever and however the tenant leaves, the tenant remains the legal owner of the items.

In many cases it will be obvious that what is left is worth little and is rubbish. In these cases, with minimal risk, you can clear everything and dispose without threat of the tenant coming back. Where there are items that make you question whether the tenant intended to leave them, such as large furniture items, a television or bicycle, it can be problematic deciding what to do with them. The question that you ask the most is: Can I dispose of all items left behind, or for how long does the landlord have to keep items left by a tenant?

The textbook answer lies in The Torts (Interference with Goods) Act 1977 (The 1977 Act). It is an old piece of legislation and is not the easiest to navigate. It provides that the landlord becomes the 'bailor' of the possessions left, effectively the guardian of the items, which is why the items remain owned by the tenant and the landlord cannot simply dispose of everything.

Several different scenarios could play out. The tenant leaves possessions which have very limited value; the tenant leaves possessions which overall seem low value but there are a few items that are more valuable; the tenant's possessions look like they have just been left in the property and not attempted to be removed. The tenancy has not been formally terminated. The landlord may or may not be owed any rent or any other monies by the tenant at the point you find the possessions.

In the first two scenarios and presuming the tenancy has ended and you have gone into the property to take legal possession, you need to make every reasonable effort to contact the tenant and establish what they intend for the items that they have left. If you can do this your job is done as either the tenant wants them, and you arrange collection, or they do not want them, and you dispose of them or sell them. Invariably, it is never as easy or neat as this (otherwise you would not need to be asking the question).

The real pain for landlords is needing to get the property let again quickly which means removing all the possessions and preparing the property for a new tenant and knowing what to do with the items to avoid costly storage charges that will inevitably end up being at the landlord's expense. This can be emotive if the landlord is owed considerable rent arrears.

To apply the textbook answer is not straightforward as The 1977 Act is tricky when it comes to providing for a clear period during which you keep the tenant's items before you can safely dispose of them. You need to take all reasonable steps to get the items back to the owner, but after twenty-eight days, or a reasonable time, you can. There is no definition of what 'reasonable steps' are, but general expectation would be to at least write to the last known address, even if that is the let property as the tenant may have a forwarding arrangement in place. You should exhaust all lines of enquiry that the referencing process may have provided – a former employer for example – and call all known phone numbers and email them, look at social media and try direct private contact (to avoid any data protection issues), instruct an enquiry agent and ask around if there is any likelihood of a possible contact with the former tenant. You need a residential address to be able to serve the notice required properly by recorded delivery.

The 1977 Act only deals with where there is an intentional storage of goods, but the landlord is an involuntary 'bailee' of goods left by a tenant as the landlord has not invited the tenant to leave them. In these cases, you would be expected to serve two notices, one requiring collection of the goods and the other a notice of intention to sell those goods. In the case of your landlord, it is best to write one letter to the tenant explaining what you would be expected to put in both notices, and you would have to serve it by recorded or special delivery. The notice period is not less than three months where the landlord as bailee is owed monies by the tenant as bailor. There are no cases to support this in lettings, and it remains a grey area. This is likely where the train of thought about a three-month longstop period of retaining the items comes from.

You will need to keep a complete audit trail to demonstrate that the expected actions set out in The 1977 Act have been taken before selling the items in question. This is to cover you if the tenant comes looking for the possessions. In most cases, if you exhaust all reasonable lines of enquiry within a month, you can safely dispose of the items. It will help to have a contractual term in the original tenancy agreement that deals with this. If the relevant clause provides fourteen days before disposal, I would be careful should there be any items of any worth and keep them a couple of weeks longer to ensure that reasonable enquiries are completed in line with the statute.

ABANDONED PROPERTY

I recall one case where an order for possession was obtained and formal eviction was required using High Court Enforcement Officers. The tenant owed thousands in rent arrears. When the agents entered the property they found a lot of possessions, though none particularly valuable. There was a sleeping bag and a lot of empty bottles of alcohol littering the attic area which suggested the tenant had been sleeping up there. The agents then discovered a suicide note and the situation became more sinister. At that point they rang me and asked for my advice. The agents reported their findings to the police though nothing further materialised, and the property was cleared within a month without repercussion.

In this scenario, you may find that the tenant has seemingly up and left midterm without giving any notice and no one has seen the tenant in a while. You enter the property to see what the situation is and find lots of possessions but nothing that suggests that anyone has lived in the property recently as there are no perishable or perished food items. If you deem the property to be abandoned by the tenant, the problem is demonstrating that the tenant intended to abandon them. You will need once again to take reasonable steps to communicate with the tenant and find out their intentions regarding the possessions left in the property and ideally whether they are returning. You then apply the twenty-eight-day period for keeping the goods before selling or disposing of them, and keep an inventory of what was left to avoid potential future issues.

The only word of warning I would give with acting based on the tenant having vacated without notice and leaving lots of possessions behind is that they may not have left. What you must be sure of is that it is highly unlikely that the tenant will return because if they were to, the landlord may be faced with an unlawful eviction claim. This may result in either a criminal or civil action against the landlord if made out.

The textbook procedure is convoluted and can be lengthy if three months' notice is necessary and can end up being expensive for the landlord. How can you work around the textbook answer? One way is to provide for such an eventuality in the tenancy agreement.

You may have an express provision in your tenancy agreement about what happens if possessions are left in the property. Like any contract term it must be worded fairly, but if you follow the similar notice periods indicated in The 1977 Act, you should be OK. You also need to phrase it so that the tenant ends up being responsible for all reasonable removal and/or storage charges when items are left in the property. It should also provide that the landlord will remove and store the items for a period of one month and will notify the tenant at the last known address. You can hold the tenant liable for the reasonable costs of disposal. Often the following words are included: 'The costs may be deducted from any sale proceeds or the deposit and if there are any costs remaining, they will remain the tenant's liability.' You may also want to avoid hanging on to junk items and provide in the tenancy that if the cost of storage is going to be greater than the value of the items in question, the landlord can dispose of those items.

Should the matter end up in court with the former tenant challenging the landlord over sale of the items, a court will consider the actions taken by the landlord as well as the wording of the clause, and the more reasonable the landlord can be shown to have been the better chance of the landlord being successful. Photographs and an inventory should be taken by way of evidence, but there will remain an element of risk of the tenant challenging the action taken if not entirely textbook or reasonable.

The Welsh government passed The Renting Homes (Wales) Act 2016 which from 1 December 2022 radically changes all sorts of rules and documents relating to tenancy agreements – or occupation agreements as they are to be called in Wales. Of note, there is a provision for possessions left behind by a tenant being stored for one month by the landlord after the end of the agreement, but only if they have some value equating to more than the storage costs. If not, then the landlord can dispose of the items immediately. This is clear and could pave the way for England to similarly follow suit with such provision becoming a standard term.

Professional protection and negotiation

No one wants to think about the possibility of something going wrong in professional practice. As human beings in a fast-paced, demanding and complex legislative environment, you need to prepare for the likelihood of a mistake so that you can focus on giving the best possible service to your clients safe in the knowledge that you are covered should the worst happen.

In most professions where an error or an omission can cause serious loss or damage, there is a requirement to have professional indemnity insurance in place. If you join a trade body such as RICS or Propertymark, you will be required to produce evidence of such insurance, but in many businesses it is usual to hold this type of insurance.

If you are a property professional with your own business, it is a legal requirement that if you employ anyone, you must have Employers' Liability Insurance in place. The focus of this cover is to protect against employees suing you for any injury or illness suffered because of working for you.

This is all regular legally required insurance cover to protect you against the risk of something unexpected happening. You may even be involved in recommending Rent Indemnity Insurance for your landlords to cover nonpayment of rent, which has been a lifeline to many landlords. This type of cover will also allow, if relevant to you, commissions to continue if rent is not paid.

What I want to explore with you are those times when you step into the role of a negotiator and may need to:

- Undertake a damage limitation exercise for you and your business due to a mistake by you or one of your employees

- Advise the best way forward for your landlord due to a deteriorating situation with their tenant

- Act against your own advice when a landlord is insistent that you do so

The above situations can leave you, respectively:

- Fighting to save your reputation

- Considering practical steps to try and save the landlord from a difficult tenancy where there seems to be no pleasing the tenant

- Wanting to protect your own back when your advice does not match what your landlord wants to do

I practise an area of law that is litigious, meaning I work with cases that involve taking a dispute to court such as a possession claim. One of the overriding principles that governs this type of work is a duty to consider whether there is any way the parties can settle their differences. Often this is unlikely in a straightforward Section 21 case where there is not any defence, but more possible in Section 8 based claims where a defence is presented for compensation for disrepair. This gives rise to the possibility of set off against the claim for rent arrears, but because the level of the compensation award is subjective and down to the court there may be a way of striking a deal to satisfy both parties without the need to go to a full trial. This can be expensive, particularly if one party is on legal aid meaning that the other party cannot recover their legal costs if they are successful. A litigator is required to draw on their skill as a negotiator during a court claim.

Suing is becoming more common, and while not every error that you make will result in a claim, you may find yourself trying to pacify your landlord without the need to go through the formal claims route using your professional indemnity insurance. With policy excesses to take account of, it may be cheaper to work on a deal with the landlord and make a payment from your own funds rather than make a claim that you must pay the excess on in any event, and which may affect your premium next year. You may find other ways around ensuring the landlord feels properly compensated for a mistake with a relaxation of a standard fee for example. A practical solution can be best in some cases rather than the formalities of the claims process, but it does depend on the seriousness of the error and likely level of compensation payable. It will depend on the facts of the case and how you are placed to make a payment if this is what it takes. What you should not lose sight of is putting your insurance company on notice. Insurance policies tend to have a strict notification procedure and short time limit after you become aware of a potential claim. Even if you do not follow the issue through to a claim because you do manage to sort it out directly with the landlord, it is best to notify rather than miss your ability to make the claim if negotiation does not prove successful.

As with any mistake, it can be costly not just to your pocket or the insurance policy, but also to the business's reputation as bad experiences are reported on far more than good ones. The faster you can communicate and resolve things with the landlord, the better.

Multiple deposit claim

An example of this is the multiple deposit claim. When there is a mistake in registering the deposit, that mistake travels on down the line of potentially statutory periodic tenancies and any renewals of the tenancy. It can lead to a multiple claim by the tenant for the penalty provided by the Housing Act 2004 for breach of the deposit regulations of one to three times the deposit. However, and here is the sting, the penalty is claimed for every new tenancy.

DEPOSIT BREACH

I had a case where there had been a mistake in the deposit requirements from a tenancy that began six years previously. The deposit breach was admitted and initially the defence and counterclaim were based on disrepair. Since the original tenancy, there had been periods of periodic tenancy then another renewal or two, then a periodic again. There was a late application to amend the counterclaim to include the multiple breaches which amounted to circa £42,000 based on the maximum of three times the deposit, on the back of what was a claim for about £16,000 of rent arrears. Starting from an admission of a breach in the deposit requirements, it escalated and swung the whole case around in favour of the tenant, though the application to amend was unsuccessful.

While there are big questions over whether this was the intention behind the drafting of the deposit regulations, it nevertheless is a valid counterclaim. It causes problems in court cases as such claims can wipe out possession claims based on rent arrears, leaving the landlord exposed to the other side's legal costs.

In this case study, the landlord made the mistake, but I have known agents get into problems due to an error or omission on the deposit paperwork, and insurance can be a lifeline if the multiple deposit claim raises its head. This can be particularly nasty if the error arose from a former agent who you may have taken over from. The indemnities agreed on that agency purchase suddenly become particularly relevant.

The tenant from hell

For example, what about the tenant from hell? You know the sort and your heart sinks. The tenant seemed charming with a perfect reference, but as soon as they move into the property, they find cause to complain about everything.

I had a case recently where despite the tenant knowing that the property had been empty for a month or two and had been – admittedly somewhat unusually – told that the property was as seen and would not be cleaned any further, the complaints about the property began as soon as the tenant stepped foot in the door. It was not just the décor and some damp; it was also the cause of illness to the tenant and tenant's family staying at the property, and they had to have numerous trips to the doctor. The tenant said they had cleaned the property but did not think it was right that it had not been cleaned, despite the express warning prior to moving in. The tenant ramped the demands up to having a full structural survey and treatment carried out, but not while they were in the property. It all sounded so grim that you questioned why the tenant was not immediately demanding to be released from the tenancy. The demands simply continued, which beat the landlord down and eventually resulted in a negotiated release as it was far easier to return the deposit and the rent for the month or so and secure vacant possession of the property than try and keep up with the daily pressure of the tenant in this case.

This is the sort of scenario that rather than me as a legal advisor getting involved could so easily have been you as the property professional taking the hit. In this case, it was easier for me to field the lengthy emails from the tenant and quickly work out that it was far better to negotiate the tenant out of the property than prolong the agony and try and keep the tenant happy for what could have been the entire length of the tenancy agreement. There is no pleasing some people and if you recognise such a person, this is when your negotiation skills are called into play, and you must do your upmost to resolve the situation for your landlord fast.

Your landlord ignores your advice

On the odd occasion, you may end up with your professional advice not being what your landlord wants to hear or take. If this happens, set out the legal position clearly in writing and any risk associated with not taking that advice, alongside what would happen if that route was not taken. Let me give you a couple of examples:

- The tenant seems to be struggling with paying the rent and has got themselves into five months of rent arrears. Your landlord asks for the deposit to be released to reduce these, but you point out the risk that the landlord has nothing to put towards any excess wear and tear when the tenant leaves. The landlord knows this but still wants to proceed and the tenant has confirmed that this can happen.

- The prospective tenant can only pass reference with a guarantor, and they are unable to find one. The landlord is willing to take the risk if the tenant can pay six months up front which the tenant is offering. You are concerned that the first six months will be paid but after that the rent may not be forthcoming and advise that this tenant is not taken on as they cannot fulfil the referencing criteria. The landlord insists that the tenant be accepted.

I expect that many of you will have faced these requests and felt your professional advice slipping away from you. As the landlord is your principal, their instructions need to be followed to avoid being outside the scope of your authority and yet following the instruction flies in the face of the risk that you would rather the landlord not take. In any such situation, I would put your professional advice in writing and ask the landlord to confirm their instructions similarly in writing. You at least have a record of what was required of you and support for the action you then took.

In some cases, as an added back up, you may decide to seek a letter of indemnity from your landlord. This is because your terms of business with the landlord are the basis of your legal relationship. If you, as one party, breach the contract the landlord as the other party may suffer loss, and this gives rise to you needing assurance that if you carry out what the landlord is wanting to do against your advice, that you will be compensated by the landlord should you suffer any loss. You seek protection from your landlord from liability, loss, claims and damages that might arise because of you carrying out what the landlord wants against your advice.

The crazy world of lettings

During the years in which I have advised on lettings law, there have been many times when I have had a good laugh about what has presented itself to you as a property professional. Numerous times I have been thankful that you are managing the property you are describing rather than me. Most memorable are the discoveries when tenants leave – the horrific conditions that you find the tenant lived in, mainly related to hygiene, the tell-tale signs of a dubious business with bottles of baby oil and tissues left about, the despair when you realise just what a hoarder the tenant was and have copious amounts of rubbish to dispose of, and the list goes on.

I thought it would be helpful, as well as being a bit of light relief, to hear some of the crazy questions and scenarios that I can recall, as each has an entirely proper legal answer or solution. Often the overwhelming situation that you discover puts pay to the rational and logical thinking required to unravel what to do next and why. While there is an element of humour initially at what may have happened, there is the stark reality for the landlord of having to put things right, and the likelihood of this being at their own expense.

I will talk about:

- Gardening

- Change of use

- The supernatural

- Hoarding

Gardening

Where there is a garden to be maintained with a property the tenancy agreement will usually say something like 'To keep the garden in the same character, weed free and in good order, and to cut the grass at reasonable intervals during the growing season'.

Questions arise from a lack of maintenance on the tenant's part and what the tenant should be responsible for. The contractual term expects a reasonable response from the tenant to keep the garden tidy and the grass cut as it needs it. According to the TDS Custodial Scheme (Tenancy Deposit Scheme), gardening accounts for over a quarter of deposit disputes and is the third most popular reason for deposit disputes.[18]

18 TDS, '#AskTDS: Maintaining gardens in rented properties – what are your responsibilities as a tenant?', Department for Levelling Up, Housing & Communities, www.tenancydepositscheme.com/asktds-maintaining-gardens-in-rented-properties-what-are-my-responsibilities-as-a-tenant, accessed 19 July 2022

There was one question which amused me which related to whether the tenant should be expected to take care of a 150-foot-high hedge. I questioned how the landlord looked after it, let alone the tenant, and that should have been enough to answer the question for the agent. The type of maintenance that requires a specialist expert to sort out is entirely unreasonable, as part of a short-term let, to be the liability of the tenant. The landlord knowing the existence and required maintenance of this hedge should factor this into the tenancy terms and ideally exclude the need to attend to such a hedge from the contract, along with any other trees or shrubs, and allow the landlord reasonable access should attention be required to it during the tenant's term.

Other questions arise from the way in which the tenant has chosen to change the garden. I have had several where hot tubs have gone in without the consent of the landlord, or a decking or patio has been built with consent but then there is confusion for the tenant over whether that should equate to monetary value at the end of the tenancy.

If a tenant chooses to carry something out without the consent of the landlord, be that in the garden or inside the property, the tenancy will usually provide for that change or alteration to be put back to how it was at the expense of the tenant. Consequently, it is not worthwhile for a short-term tenant to spend money on a property that they will not ultimately benefit from other than during the time they occupy that property. The tenant will pay for the change as well as the cost to change it back.

Some landlords are willing to allow their tenants to carry out certain work, but this needs to be very carefully expressed as a special term of the tenancy to avoid any confusion over who was responsible for the cost later and whether the change needs to be reversed at the end of the tenant's term.

In the hot tub scenario, the tenant had no consent from the landlord to hard landscape the garden and put the hot tub in, and then totally misunderstood the legal position when they tried to claim thousands of pounds for the changes to the garden. Their threat to remove the hot tub was no threat and, in fact, entirely acceptable to the landlord provided the garden was put back to how the tenant found it when they first moved in.

Change of use

The standard terms of a residential tenancy agreement relating to the use of the property to:

- Use the Premises for the purpose of a private residence only in the occupation of the Tenant and not for business purposes

- Not use the Premises for any illegal, immoral or improper use

- Not use or consume in or about the Premises during the continuance of this tenancy any drugs mentioned in the Misuse of Drugs Act 1971 or any other controlled substances, the use of which may from this time on be prohibited or restricted by statute

There have been illegal changes of use over the years, from the rise in tenants turning properties into an Airbnb to a basement being turned into a dominatrix-themed dungeon. One of the most devastating for landlords is a tenant turning the property into a cannabis farm. The cannabis plant thrives indoors with twenty-four-hour a day lighting and water, carbon dioxide and humidity, all of which can be produced in a residential property with some adaptations and which from the outside continues to look like a regular residential abode. The worst sort of tenant will strip out the insides of the property and dedicate it to the growing of the cannabis plants. On one occasion I recall the clue that something irregular was going on was the amateur group of wires dangling from the property and being connected shoddily to a nearby lamppost for the illicit supply of the consistent electricity needed. Cannabis is a controlled substance. Clues of a problem may be the smell that emanates from the plants, lights on all day and all night, condensation on windows or the sound of ventilation fans which are usually on twenty-four hours a day, seven days a week. If the alarm bells start ringing, call the police immediately and do not contact any of the tenants.

The cost to put the property back to its original state can be significant and malicious damage such as this by a tenant may not be covered by insurance. If insurance does there is often a maximum that the policy will pay out.

It is this sort of terrible eventuality that often provides you as a property professional, with your thorough referencing service, the chance to act on behalf of such landlords.

The supernatural

This can be a tough one, as most of you, unsurprisingly, are not too sure whether to think that the tenant reporting having seen a ghost is trying to pull a fast one to get out of the tenancy, is hallucinating due to drug misuse or there is some supernatural force at work which you are required to do something about, and, if so, what exactly? If you choose to ignore such a claim, the question is whether you are causing a breach of the tenant's covenant of quiet enjoyment, whether you believe it or not. Depending on the facts, it might be worth offering to seek advice from a medium or the like to look willing in the first instance, but beyond this – subject to the findings – a landlord cannot do much more. If the tenant does try and terminate the tenancy early, usual rules apply without any proof of a reason that the property is now uninhabitable, so early release or surrender.

Hoarding

I want to mention at this juncture a much more sobering but very serious issue that must be handled carefully and is becoming more prevalent. It can be very distressing for landlords and neighbours of the property in question: hoarding.

This is a mental health disorder and can cause dreadful problems in a rented property including fire risks due to rubbish being everywhere, the inability to carry out any form of inspection and problems with vermin due to excessive rubbish in the garden or outer area of the premises. This is a difficult issue to cope with as despite the large number of possessions the tenant will find it difficult or impossible to throw things away. There have been a few television programmes about people trying to cope with this disorder, and it is hard to watch. You may need to try and secure the support from next of kin or a mental health support worker.

Reports of this in properties are on the increase and some tenants are known to the local council and fire service in terms of environmental impact as they have assessed the property enough times often due to neighbours' concerns. You may receive reports of problems from neighbours or realise the issue when you attempt to carry out an interim property inspection.

What you as a property professional must know is that hoarding is classed as a disability under Section 6(1) of the Equality Act 2010, in that it is a physical or mental impairment, and the impairment has a substantial long-term adverse effect on that person's ability to carry out normal day-to-day activities. A private landlord cannot discriminate on the grounds of disability when they are making an offer to let a property. If a tenant raises a defence of disability discrimination under the Equality Act during a claim for possession, it will be up to the landlord to show that the eviction is justified. An eviction must be a proportionate means of achieving the aim and landlords must be more considerate towards a disabled tenant. Allowance must be given due to the tenant's disability, and this can make it trickier, but not impossible, to secure possession.

To round this section off I would like to mention a deed of surrender that had to be prepared a short while ago between a client landlord and a tenant. It was all agreed, though it had been difficult to get the tenant to agree to go, and when the deed was sent to the tenant for a witnessed signature the tenant's demand before signing off was memorable. Before executing the deed, the tenant insisted that the landlord buy his wife a birthday cake and some balloons. By that stage the landlord found this to be the least of his worries and duly did so to ensure the end to the matter.

Easy areas of law to get right

As professionals, you and I expect to be held to account for the work undertaken. Whether as part of a business or the owner of a business, the clients come first to ensure they receive the best possible service. When a profession is fully regulated the expectation for a great service is high and that is the position in the legal sector. As a property professional, you are largely unregulated, for the moment at least, and yet you are increasingly held to account for numerous parts of legislation that govern the private rented sector. With the principal aim to make the lettings process as fair as possible for everyone, you must be alert to the numerous relevant legal areas, some of which I have mentioned, and the regular changes to remain compliant.

Compliance is attractive to your landlord clients and a great selling point. It is stressful for landlords to keep up with the changes, and many want to focus on other things of interest rather than investment properties. Appointing a professional to stay compliant on their behalf throughout the lettings process and to deal with everything that entails, provides a wonderful platform to off-load the compliance burden. It is not just about managing their property but more investing in you to manage the twists and turns of the many legal aspects of letting that property. What better way to market your business than as fully compliant?

I have looked at areas where your legal questions are prominent and why. Here I look at the law which you should find much easier to be compliant with and why, and what legal issues have arisen where appropriate. A compliance-savvy letting agent is what you are aiming for, but to gain real success you must be able to let your ideal landlords know just what a vast array of compliance you must deal with and why the best option for them is to employ you.

For a large part, I have focused on the law surrounding letting a property. I now turn to the two other main areas important to you, including:

- How to keep your agency compliant

- Preparation of the property to be let

Whether you are the owner or an employee, you need to be well-versed in agency compliance to get the most from it and attract customers. There are a few legal 'must haves' for a letting agent business.

Client money protection

Embedded in the Housing and Planning Act 2016, and brought in by The Client Money Protection Schemes for Property Agents (Requirement to Belong to a Scheme etc) Regulations 2019 as amended by the Tenant Fees Act 2019, all property agents in England since 1 April 2019 (transition period ended 1 April 2021) holding client money must be members of a government-approved client money protection scheme.

Why? There were too many cases of agencies going into administration or misappropriating landlord and tenant funds. The scheme became a mandatory requirement to protect landlords and tenants and allow them to be compensated if their money cannot be repaid, be that wholly or in part. It is about boosting confidence and trust in you as agents.

Redress scheme membership

Since 1 October 2014 under the statutory instrument entitled The Redress Scheme for Lettings Agency Work and Property Management Work (Requirement to Belong to a Scheme etc) (England) Order 2014 No. 2359, you must join one of two schemes – Property Redress Scheme or The Property Ombudsman (TPO) – and agree to use that resolution process should there be a complaint against you by one of your landlords. This is a consumer rights-based scheme, and you must accept the outcome of decisions made.

Why? This was designed to be an outlet for consumer complaints about your service. It makes it easier to resolve issues that may arise cost effectively and without the need to use the courts.

General Data Protection Regulation

The General Data Protection Regulation (GDPR) was implemented despite the UK leaving the European Union by the Data Protection Act 2018. GDPR concerns the use and storage of personal information handled by you and your business. You must follow strict rules known as 'data protection principles' to ensure that the information is used fairly, lawfully and transparently; is used for specified purposes; is accurate; is held no longer than necessary; and is securely handled. Consumers must know how their data will be used and be able to erase it in some circumstances or update it among other rights.

Why? This prevents the data that you handle from being misused by third parties for fraud, like phishing scams and identity theft.

Money laundering

Letting agency business came into the scope of Money Laundering Regulations on 10 January 2020. Money Laundering and Terrorist Financing (Amendment) Regulations 2019 require those falling under the definition of letting agency activity and who deal with any property that meets the rent threshold of €10,000 or more per month for the duration of at least a month to register with Her Majesty's Revenue and Customs (HMRC) and follow the anti-money laundering regulations. If you are the business owner, you must pass the approval checks before your business can register with HMRC, and this is a legal requirement to trade.

Why? You are deemed to be a medium risk for the likelihood of money being laundered through your business, and you could be liable for a civil penalty or criminal prosecution should you fail to comply with the regulations.

Consumer Rights Act 2015

From 27 May 2015 letting agents have had a duty to publish a list of their 'relevant' fees in accordance with Section 83 of this Act. Section 85 of the Act defines the relevant fees.

The list must be displayed prominently at every office operated by the agent where you deal face to face with persons using or proposing to use the services to which the fees relate. Specific information to make the fees clear is required, including a fee and figure inclusive of VAT, a full description of the fee to be easily understood as to what the fee applies to and covers and to ensure clarity as to whether the fee applies to the property as a whole or to each tenant.

Why? This makes it much clearer and more transparent as to what fees will be incurred by anyone considering entering a contract with you. The fees issue has been a constant area of complaint about agents, and this rule, along with the more recent Tenant Fees Act 2019, address this problem. The list of fees must also be on your website.

You demonstrate a desire to be recognised as a business that values its customers by displaying in your windows and on your website the various logos or stickers that represent your compliance with these legally required aspects to letting property.

I am still taking instructions from landlords whose former agents misappropriated funds and are under criminal investigation for fraud. Whilst you may think compliance is a must for the industry that you are in, there are some who think it is acceptable to ignore it. The landlords I deal with are all out of pocket having had at the least to find the deposit that the former agent failed to register. The landlords risk being sued for one to three times the deposit for breach of the regulations, especially as I often advise them to return the deposit to serve a valid Section 21 notice required to gain possession of their property. These are not professional landlords, and the stress of the situation can be apparent to the health of the landlord involved. There is also the rent that has not been properly accounted for to the landlord which is effectively 'lost' as the tenant is not liable to pay it twice. All payments, despite the investigations of the 'rogue agent', are highly unlikely to be recovered.

Preparation and checks

Preparation is based around ensuring the fundamental safety of the property to those who will occupy it or visit it. Keeping tenants safe is at the heart of letting property. There are various contract terms that are implied into residential tenancy agreements relating to safety including the Occupiers Liability Act 1984 and Section 11 of the Landlord and Tenant Act 1985 relating to repair of certain installations. These terms apply even if you fail to mention them in your tenancy agreement.

Section 1 of the Homes (Fitness for Human Habitation) Act 2018 has been in place since 20 March

2019 and requires that any dwelling in England is fit for human habitation at the time the tenancy is granted, or the start of the term if this is later and will remain fit throughout the term of the tenancy. This is the starting point for all properties being let, and coupled with using the checklist that local authorities would use if a tenant complained about their property being sub-standard under the Housing Health and Safety Rating System, you should be able to ensure the property meets the necessary safety standards before you let it.

There are the more familiar checks associated with energy efficiency (EPC), gas, fire and electrical safety, and the Legionella Risk Assessments linking to the water supply.

Let me take you briefly through the requirements for the checks, indicate the main reasons why they are so important to comply with in addition to simply keeping the tenant safe, and finish with a look at a few areas where your legal questions arise.

Energy Performance Certificate

An EPC, as it is commonly called, has been a legal requirement for residential property that is built, sold or let before the property is marketed since October 2008. The certificate is designed to indicate how much it will cost to heat and power a property and provides an energy efficiency rating graded from A to G. Every certificate is valid for ten years. They are all virtual and can be found by searching Finding an Energy Certificate on www.gov.uk.

Since 1 October 2018 new tenancies have had to have an EPC of no less than an E rating, and since 1 October 2020 all tenancies have had to have this E rating. There are exemptions to the requirement, and these must be registered (eg, when all relevant improvements have been made but the property cannot be improved to an E).

With energy such a prominent area of discussion, the plans are for the rating to be increased to a C for new tenancies by December 2025 and all tenancies by 2028.

Importance: For tenancies commencing on or after 1 October 2015, an EPC must have been served on the tenant prior to a Section 21 notice being served to ensure the notice is valid. You must be able to show when and how it was served on the tenant.

Gas safety certificate

The Gas Safety (Installations and Use) Regulations 1998 govern the requirement for a gas safe engineer to check properties with a gas supply and its fixed and portable gas appliances and flues on a yearly basis. A copy of the certificate must be given to the tenant before they move into the property and within twenty-eight days of all further gas safety checks being made throughout the duration of the tenancy.

Importance: For tenancies commencing on or after 1 October 2015, a valid gas safety certificate (this can be the most recent valid one) must be served on the tenant prior to a Section 21 notice being served.

Fire safety

The Smoke and Carbon Monoxide Alarm (England) Regulations 2015 require landlords to have a working smoke alarm on every floor of their properties and a carbon monoxide alarm in any room containing a solid fuel burning appliance. From 1 October 2022, the regulations are extended to cover carbon monoxide alarms in any room where there is a fixed combustion appliance, which includes a gas boiler.

Fire safety is of particular importance in HMOs, but equally in flats where fire doors need to be fitted and must be self-closing if on corridors and staircases.

Importance: You must test that the alarms work at the start of each tenancy. Flats need more vigilance when it comes to ensuring communal areas are not blocked. This area is being further developed considering the Grenfell Tower tragedy and there will be more onus on fire assessment for properties, including the Building Safety Act 2022.

Electrical Installation Condition Report

Section 122 of Housing and Planning Act 2016 paved the way for the introduction of the Electrical Safety

Standards in the Private Rented Sector (England) Regulations 2020 which brought in the legal requirement from 1 June 2020 that an electrical installation condition report (EICR) be commissioned for every new tenancy from that date. This extended to all tenancies in existence from 1 April 2021 to ensure all relevant properties have a report which must be carried out every five years.

This is the first mandatory requirement for electrical testing and checks in residential let property and must be carried out by a competent engineer. The report refers to codes C1–C3 where C1 and C2 categories are failures and must be dealt with within twenty-eight days of them being reported. The report must be given to the tenant at the start of all new tenancies.

Importance: This was a significant step for electrical safety in let properties and to many one which was long overdue. If the report shows C1s and C2s the work must be carried out ideally before the tenant enters the property. C3s are recommendations and do not have to be carried out but should be monitored if not attended to.

Legionella risk assessment

Under the Health and Safety at Work Act 1974, landlords have a legal duty to ensure that they assess and control the risk associated with tenants being exposed to legionella bacteria. You do not have to procure a recognised testing certificate, and therefore it is an assessment, but one which you should undertake at the outset of each new tenancy. You need to ensure that someone who knows what they are looking for undertakes the check, and this can be someone in your office with no special qualification required.

Importance: To check that the risk of legionella bacteria in the water supply remains low, which it tends to be in most residential settings. Basic actions include flushing out the water system for several minutes before using, particularly if the property has been empty a while. Also, where there is a water tank, ensuring no debris gets into the water supply.

These are the most relevant of the compliance areas facing you as you set up your business as well as each property you are letting. There is much more to each than I have covered here, and these areas change and extend from time to time, so it is essential to keep a watch on them. Most legal questions arise from the transition periods that are provided for the implementation of new parts of regulations, such as that with the new EICR and the new energy rating levels for EPCs. These are valid questions as the dates and timings can prove problematic, particularly as you have no choice but to apply the textbook to all matters of compliance as practical solutions will not make you compliant or may result in possible penalties for not being.

A stronger business from your legal questions

When you work in a business, you want to develop into a stronger professional from a personal perspective. If you own the business, you want this for you and your staff as this will pave the way to a stronger business. In this chapter, I have looked at evaluating and where possible reducing the risks associated with the work you do daily and making decisions and advising your landlord about the best practical way to resolve a situation rather than always the strict legal one. You need to know when it is right to take a risk but also allow any staff members to know that if they happen to get something wrong, there is indemnity cover available. There is reassurance that you have protected the business and them adequately, allowing the work environment to be as safe as it can be in this regard. You should advocate that everyone speaks up if they recognise a mistake has been made, but it is a learning exercise once the error is known.

Your legal questions are constantly supporting a fluid and developing workplace but put the HOUSE rules in place for each property professional implementing any lettings law and suddenly you have the overarching scaffold to build that stronger business.

Imagine if whenever a legal question arose it was talked about initially and team knowledge utilised to answer it: Highlight ✓

Imagine if the question you asked was not one you could answer between yourselves, but solely or with others you thought about it until you were confident you had the right clear question to get the required answer: **O**ptimise ✓

Imagine uncovering the legal answer and understanding the relevant law that you wanted easily and concisely from conversing with a legal advisor: **U**ncover ✓

Imagine sharing the answer with everyone back in the office feeling great that you found out and can move that matter on, but knowing it is far more useful for everyone to know it rather than only you: **S**hare ✓

Imagine that you, possibly with the business owner, found the time to work on and evaluate what procedures might be changed or what processes could be implemented or amended to support the answer: **E**valuate ✓

Application of the HOUSE rules brings meaning and purpose to asking questions. They should encourage you to ask legal questions in a way that can guide you to getting something from the answers most, if not all, of the time. It will certainly improve confidence across the business and is a process that can easily be discussed in meetings to see if everyone is working in a uniform and positive way to support the business with the legal issues as they arise.

If, for example, the same legal question is being raised again and again despite what seems regular discussion on the subject, it may be time to get some training in place so there is a better understanding of the legal issue. For the reasons I explored in Chapter

Five, your basic legal knowledge may require a bolster before the understanding sinks in.

A stronger business probably means slightly different things to everyone, but generally to ensure the meaningful use of your legal answers you will need to:

- Be organised – get everyone using the HOUSE rules and let everyone know where to record and/or find answers

- Keep detailed records of action taken with the legal answer or processes to be implemented as a result

- Ensure everyone is aware of the risks in areas of your work and how this should be dealt with, perhaps with a second opinion before action is taken if not a textbook answer

- Get proactive and creative with the legal answers to remember them and ensure everyone else can too, whether by flow charts or processes in creation of documents

- Keep your focus as legal questions can be time well spent with the HOUSE rules applied – ensure clarity in the question and you will get the right answer

- Give excellent service, which you will as you will be confident with your legal answers in front of your clients

- Keep an eye on the competition – what are they doing and is it worth doing too

If the legal answer was not one you wanted to hear, it is likely that you will learn more from it than any other answer as it will stick clearly in your mind.

I recall one issue for an agent who had taken on the management of a property from a former agent, and it related to the change-over of the deposit. The old agent delayed getting the deposit released, so the new agent registered the deposit with their chosen deposit scheme as it was an insured scheme. The deposit was eventually received, but it was a couple of months later, and the new agent forgot to serve the updated prescribed information and scheme leaflet until several months after that. The tenants left the property and sued the landlord for three times the deposit for not getting the change-over of the deposit right.

I felt for the new agent as there is no specific regulation that deals with change of agent in the Housing Act 2004, and yet it seemed obvious that there had been a breach, and good practice dictates that given that this is a change to the way the tenant's deposit is held and a change to the original tenancy contract, you should get the consent to the change from the tenant before you take action. The thirty days would be the likely start point for the judge considering this if a claim had been taken (it was settled out of court), so it was not worth the risk of a claim being brought and the matter settled very reasonably.

With this scenario a stricter application of the usual rules would have been a better bet. These things happen and the agent was covered by insurance if they needed to use it, and I know that they will be extra careful should they take on a property from a former agent again. Ideally, this legal answer will have become an integral part of their procedures whenever there is a change of agent to them, detailing how the deposit must be treated and the documents to be served and when.

Summary

In some legal situations you have choice – whether to apply the textbook answer or a practical solution for your landlord. Commit to using the HOUSE rules for all your legal questions and build a stronger business. Make sure to:

- Weigh up the risk for each decision you make

- Consider the implications for the landlord if the risk is too high

- Consider whether the costs are prohibitive if the strict legal route is followed, and if it might be better to take a risk and have the issue resolved out of court using the cost saved

- Ensure you have the right insurance protection in place to alleviate pressure on you for mistakes that may occur

- Remember there is a legal basis for the scenario you face, however crazy it seems

- Get the easy compliance areas right and ensure that you and all those in your business know how to promote the business because you are so compliant

Conclusion

My aim is to inspire you to adopt a new way to approach asking legal questions and encourage you to continue your learning journey from the questions you need answers to. You have knowledge of the commonly asked questions raised by those in the industry, and as an initial easy step you should be keen to examine how you deal with those answers within your own workplace.

The HOUSE rules are my gift to you whenever you need to ask a question, and, like every new habit or rule, you will need to remind yourself of them initially and soon it will be an automatic application. HOUSE is an obvious and easy acronym to remember, and relevantly linked to you as a property professional applying lettings law. This book can be used as a reference or prompt to embed the rules, and I have every confidence it will become second nature in a short time.

You will be:

- Highlighting legal issues

- Optimising those questions to ensure the clarity and need to get the right question asked

- Uncovering and upholding the law with the legal answers you receive

- Sharing the answers to get the most from them

- Evaluating how best to embed the answers simply and effectively into your working practices to ensure legal compliance for you and everyone you work with

I know that there will be those of you thinking that it is all easier said than done, and that it seems like a lot of effort. To make a smart change to your career as a property professional, you should be gravitating towards using business tools that allow you to develop your full potential and become the success you are working for quickly. The HOUSE rules are nothing but supportive of this purpose, and it only involves recalling five letters when you need to ask a legal question.

Knowing how often the same sort of questions are asked, the HOUSE rules can improve your understanding and reduce the time wasted in duplicating questions and only using that answer for that one scenario without a thought for anyone else that might benefit from the answer. Not only would repeating the answer to your colleagues reinforce your grasp of the law, but it would also support your business and possibly create a new process to avoid the same problem again.

With the regular changes of legislation within the private rented sector, there is every reason to get good at asking questions about lettings law and to use your answers appropriately to build confidence in you individually and to benefit your business. Impressing and supporting landlords is a key benefit of the HOUSE rules and adoption of this simple process is at your fingertips.

I have produced a free downloadable prompt sheet with details of how you can properly prepare to ask questions on various subjects. Simply visit www.duttongregory.co.uk/site/commercial/landlord-and-tenant to make use of this resource. You will also find a HOUSE rules reminder page to help embody the thought process for using the rules. Consider keeping it to hand.

Your legal questions are a fantastic asset to your personal and business development and accomplishments. Shape your questions as the HOUSE rules intend and with the sharing and evaluating of your answers you can build a strong foundation from which to enrich your career and excel in business.

Glossary Of Acronyms

ARLA   Association of Residential Letting Agents

AST   Assured Shorthold Tenancy, as defined by Housing Act 1988, Section 1

EICR   Electrical Installation Condition Report

EPC   Energy Performance Certificate

GDPR   General Data Protection Regulation

HMO   House in Multiple Occupation

HMRC   Her Majesty's Revenue and Customs

HOUSE   Highlight, Optimise, Uncover, Share, Evaluate

NALS   National Approved Letting Scheme – now Safeagent

NEA	National Association of Estate Agents
NHA	Non-Housing Act tenancy (or common law tenancy)
PAS	Primary Authority Scheme
PRS	Property Redress Scheme
RICS	Royal Institution of Chartered Surveyors
RoPA	Regulation of Property Agents
TDS	Tenancy Deposit Scheme
TOB	Terms of Business
TPO	The Property Ombudsman
VOA	Valuation Office Agency

Further Information And Resources

Referenced legislation

You can find the relevant legislation by visiting www. legislation.gov.uk.

Title	Year and Number	Legislation Type
Distress for Rent Act 1737	1737 c 19	Act of the Parliament of Great Britain
Law of Property Act 1925	1925 c 25	UK Public General Act
Powers of Attorney Act 1971	1971 c 27	UK Public General Act
Misuse of Drugs Act 1971	1971 c 38	UK Public General Act

Title	Year and Number	Legislation Type
Health and Safety at Work etc Act 1974	1974 c 37	UK Public General Act
Torts (Interference with Goods) Act 1977	1977 c 32	UK Public General Act
Rent Act 1977	1977 c 42	UK Public General Act
Protection From Eviction Act 1977	1977 c 43	UK Public General Act
Housing Act 1980	1980 c 51	UK Public General Act
Landlord and Tenant Act 1985	1985 c 70	UK Public General Act
Housing Act 1988	1988 c 50	UK Public General Act
The Gas Safety (Installations and Use) Regulations 1998	1998 No 2451	UK Statutory Instrument
The Unfair Terms in Consumer Contracts Regulations 1999	1999 No 2083	UK Statutory Instrument
The Electronic Communications Act 2000	2000 c 7	UK Public General Act
Housing Act 2004	2004 c 34	UK Public General Act
Consumer Protection from Unfair Trading Regulations	2008 No 1277	UK Statutory Instrument
Equality Act 2010	2010 c 15	UK Public General Act
Immigration Act 2014	2014 c 22	UK Public General Act

Title	Year and Number	Legislation Type
The Redress Scheme for Lettings Agency Work and Property Management Work (Requirement to Belong to A Scheme, etc) (England) Order 2014 No 2359	2014 No 2359	UK Statutory Instrument
Consumer Rights Act 2015	2015 c 15	UK Public General Act
The Smoke and Carbon Monoxide Alarm (England) Regulations 2015	2015 No 1693	UK Statutory Instrument
The Smoke and Carbon Monoxide Alarm (Amendment) Regulations 2022	2022 No 707	UK Statutory Instrument
Immigration Act 2016	2016 c 19	UK Public General Act
Housing and Planning Act 2016	2016 c 22	UK Public General Act
Renting Homes (Wales) Act 2016	2016 anaw 1	Act of the National Assembly for Wales
Data Protection Act 2018	2018	UK Public General Act
Homes (Fitness for Human Habitation) Act 2018	2018 c 34	UK Public General Act
The Money Laundering and Terrorist Financing (Amendment) Regulations 2019	2019 No 1511	UK Statutory Instrument

Title	Year and Number	Legislation Type
The Client Money Protection Schemes for Property Agents (Requirement to Belong to a Scheme etc) Regulations 2019	2019 No 386	UK Statutory Instrument
Tenant Fees Act 2019	2019 c 4	UK Public General Act
Electrical Safety Standards in The Private Rented Sector (England) Regulations 2020	2020 No 312	UK Statutory Instrument
The Renting Homes (Fitness for Human Habitation) (Wales) Regulations 2022	2022 No 6 (W 4)	Wales Statutory Instrument

Useful links

- **Right to Rent procedure**: www.gov.uk/check-tenant-right-to-rent-documents

- **Intestacy Rules Chart – 'Choice not Chance'**: https://assets.publishing.service.gov.uk/government/uploads/system/uploads/attachment_data/file/415873/choice-not-chance-flow-chart.pdf

- **Rent Smart Wales licence**: www.rentsmart.gov.wales/en/licensing

- **Private Rented Sector Code of Best Practice (The Property Redress Scheme)**: www.theprs.co.uk/ Resource/ViewFile/34

- **The Property Ombudsman (TPO)**: www.tpos. co.uk

- **Code of Practice for Residential Lettings Agents (England), set by The Property Ombudsman (TPO)**: www.tpos.co.uk/images/documents/ Codes/TPOE22-7_Code_of_Practice_for_ Residential_Letting_Agents_A4_FINAL.pdf

Acknowledgements

I would like to thank all those property professionals who over many years have asked legal lettings questions and who have effectively contributed to and influenced the subject matter for this book.

My thanks particularly to Mark Chatterton for his challenging questions and professional support; to Robert Bolwell who I have worked with for years and whose wisdom I have valued on occasions too numerous to mention; to Ryan Heaven for his enthusiasm for the work we do; to Charlotte Howard and Zaza Oswald whose legal knowledge and lettings expertise I greatly respect and whose friendships I cherish; to my brother-in-law Mark Riddleston for his fantastic contribution; and to my husband Tony Peters who read the book but would have been happier bringing the book to life with his artistic skills.

Thank you to Susannah Brade-Waring and Karin Karian who as my business and voice coaches respectively have unleashed the creative part in me and given me the confidence to bring my authentic self into being.

To Daniel Priestley for his fabulous business books which have propelled me to write, and ReThink Press whose BookBuilder course and publishing expertise have allowed me to achieve more than I ever imagined.

Thank you also to my partners and colleagues at Dutton Gregory Solicitors who collectively have been the steady base from which I have been able to sharpen my legal knowledge and become the solicitor I am over the years. I am hugely proud of and wholeheartedly thank my current Landlord and Tenant Team and all those who have worked with me as part of it over the years. Your knowledge has and continues to positively support so many letting agents.

The Author

Gina Peters qualified as a solicitor in October 1995 and has spent her legal career in private practice along the South Coast of England. With a love of resolving legal problems combined with court process and rules, Gina developed her expertise in civil litigation. Gina worked for six years as a general civil litigation solicitor and then specialised in residential housing law. Since November 2001, she has practised at Dutton Gregory Solicitors, becoming an equity partner in July 2017. Gina successfully led the sizeable landlord and tenant team to the respected position it holds today. Her legal knowledge supports private landlords, letting agents and rent indemnity insurers together with those companies developing and operating prop tech to support the industry.

☐ http://linkedin.com/in/gina-peters-a949632b

☐ www.facebook.com/profile.
php?id=100077561619663

☐ @ginaLandTHOUSE